TACO NIGHT!

TACO NIGHT!

101 FIESTA-WORTHY RECIPES FOR DINNER FROM QUESADILLAS TO BURRITOS & TACOS PLUS DRINKS, SIDES & DESSERTS!

OXMOOR HOUSE®

CONTENTS

WELCOME

Make tonight *Taco Night!*

When you want a fun dinner the entire family will love, it's *Taco Night!* There's something festive about putting out the "fixings" for a taco bar that appeals to everyone. While the mild tasters may skip the jalapeños, the bold ones can layer on the heat. The kids can have their pick of the toppings as well, allowing everyone to be excited about their favorite south-of-the-border meals!

Whether you're hungry for soft tacos, hearty enchiladas, or sizzling fajitas, you'll find them in Tacos Deliciosos and Mexican Dinners. Classic Guacamole (page 9) is sure to become a staple, whether using it for burritos, salads, or even as a sandwich spread, but don't overlook our other guacamoles and salsas to meet your family's tastes. Or, when in a hurry, simply pick up prepared toppings at your grocery for a quick start to the meal.

Check out the "Little Helpers" boxes, offering clever ways for kids to join in, making *Taco Night!* a fun experience for the whole family. Plus, there's an entire chapter of kid-friendly finger foods, including their favorite quesadillas. You'll also find tips for even faster ways to make each dish along with ways to add more flavor to spice it up! Add a festive side or a scrumptious dessert, and you'll be ready to say, "Olé!"

Arriba Appetizers

Start off dinner
with an "Olé!"
and some of these great
drinks, dips, and small bites.

CLASSIC GUACAMOLE

makes: 8 servings hands-on time: 10 min. total time: 10 min.

Packed with fresh tomatoes and cilantro, this crowd favorite is an essential for taco night.

4 **medium avocados, pitted and peeled**

2 **large tomatoes, chopped (2 cups)**

1 **cup chopped red onion**

¼ **cup chopped fresh cilantro**

1 **Tbsp. lime zest**

¼ **cup fresh lime juice**

1 **jalapeño pepper, seeded and chopped**

½ **tsp. table salt**

1. Mash avocados with a fork in a large bowl.

2. Stir in remaining ingredients until well blended. Serve, or cover and refrigerate up to 30 minutes.

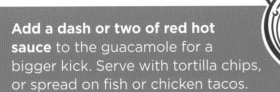

Taco Tip

Add a dash or two of red hot sauce to the guacamole for a bigger kick. Serve with tortilla chips, or spread on fish or chicken tacos.

FRESH ORANGE GUACAMOLE

makes: 8 servings hands-on time: 15 min. total time: 1 hour, 15 min.

Serve this versatile dip as an appetizer, or add a gourmet touch to a casual taco bar any day of the week.

4   ripe avocados, halved

1   large navel orange, peeled, sectioned, and cut into ½-inch pieces

2   Tbsp. finely chopped red onion

3   Tbsp. fresh orange juice

1   jalapeño pepper, seeded and finely chopped

1   garlic clove, pressed

¾   tsp. table salt

Tortilla chips

Garnish: fresh pomegranate seeds

1. Scoop avocado pulp into a bowl; mash with a fork just until chunky.

2. Stir in orange and next 5 ingredients. Cover and chill 1 to 4 hours.

GLUTEN-FREE DIP!

BLACK BEAN AND CORN SALSA

makes: 24 servings hands-on time: 10 min. total time: 10 min.

This spicy salsa is great spooned over beef or fish tacos for an extra layer of flavor.

- **2 (15-oz.) cans black beans, drained and rinsed**
- **2 (14½-oz.) cans fire-roasted diced tomatoes, drained**
- **1 (11-oz.) can chipotle white corn, drained**
- **¼ cup chopped fresh cilantro**
- **1 chipotle chile in adobo sauce (from 7-oz. can), chopped**
- **2 Tbsp. fresh lime juice**
- **½ tsp. table salt**

1. Combine all ingredients in a large bowl. Serve immediately, or refrigerate until serving time.

You can also use frozen white corn instead of canned. Add adobo sauce to taste (from chipotle can).

Taco Tip

READY IN 10 MINUTES!

GRILLED CORN SALSA

makes: about 6 cups hands-on time: 25 min. total time: 35 min.

This is a great fresh-tasting salsa, and it's very convenient if you've already got the grill preheated for cooking taco meats.

3   ears fresh corn, husks removed

Vegetable cooking spray

1   tsp. table salt

½   tsp. black pepper

3   medium tomatoes, seeded and chopped

2   jalapeño peppers, seeded and finely chopped

2   (15-oz.) cans black beans, drained and rinsed

¾   cup chopped fresh cilantro

⅓   cup fresh lime juice

2   Tbsp. chopped fresh mint

2   avocados

1. Preheat grill to 350° to 400° (medium-high) heat. Lightly coat corn cobs with cooking spray. Sprinkle with salt and pepper.

2. Grill corn, covered with grill lid, 15 to 20 minutes or until golden brown, turning every 5 minutes. Remove from grill; cool 15 minutes.

3. Hold each grilled cob upright on a cutting board; carefully cut downward, cutting kernels from cob. Discard cobs; place kernels in a large bowl. Gently stir in tomatoes and next 5 ingredients. Cover and chill until ready to serve, if desired.

4. If chilled, let corn mixture stand at room temperature 30 minutes. Peel and chop avocados; toss with corn mixture just before serving.

FRESH SALSA

makes: about 4 cups hands-on time: 15 min. total time: 15 min.

This salsa is so simple and requires no cooking—just coarsely chop and whirl in the food processor.

¼ **medium-size sweet onion**

1 **small garlic clove, quartered**

1 **jalapeño pepper, seeded and quartered**

¼ **cup loosely packed fresh cilantro leaves**

2 **lb. tomatoes**

1 **lime**

1¼ **tsp. table salt**

1. Coarsely chop onion. Pulse onion and next 3 ingredients in a food processor until finely chopped.

2. Cut each tomato into 4 pieces. Cut core from each piece; discard core. Add tomatoes to food processor in batches, and pulse each batch until well blended.

3. Transfer to a large bowl. Squeeze juice from lime over salsa, and stir in salt.

Taco Tip

By seeding the jalapeños, you're adding great flavor with just a bit of spice. Make this salsa spicier by leaving in the seeds.

EASY & FRESH!

SPICY QUESO DIP

makes: about 3 cups hands-on time: 20 min. total time: 20 min.

Now you can make this restaurant favorite at home. Who knew it took just a little sautéing and microwaving to make this indulgent dip?

1 **small onion, diced**

1 **Tbsp. oil**

1 **garlic clove, minced**

1 **(16-oz.) package processed pepper Jack cheese, cubed**

1 **(10-oz.) can diced tomatoes and green chiles**

2 **Tbsp. chopped fresh cilantro**

1. Cook onion in hot oil in a large nonstick skillet over medium-high heat 8 minutes or until tender. Add garlic, and cook 1 minute. Remove from heat.

2. Combine cheese, tomatoes, and onion mixture in a large microwave-safe glass bowl. Microwave at HIGH 5 minutes, stirring every 2½ minutes. Stir in cilantro.

Note: We tested with Velveeta® Pepper Jack.

HOT & BUBBLY!

HOT TEX-MEX PIMIENTO CHEESE DIP

makes: 16 servings hands-on time: 10 min. total time: 35 min.

1½ cups mayonnaise

½ (12-oz.) jar roasted red bell peppers, drained and chopped

¼ cup chopped green onions (4 medium)

1 jalapeño pepper, seeded and finely chopped

2 cups (8 oz.) shredded extra-sharp Cheddar cheese

2 cups (8 oz.) shredded pepper Jack cheese

Garnish: chopped fresh cilantro

French bread slices

1. Preheat oven to 350°. Spray 9-inch round (2-qt.) glass baking dish with cooking spray.

2. Mix mayonnaise, roasted peppers, green onions, and jalapeño pepper in a large bowl; stir in cheeses. Spoon mixture into baking dish.

3. Bake, uncovered, at 350° for 20 to 25 minutes or until golden and bubbly. Serve dip warm with bread slices.

You can also bake this dip in 2 (1-qt.) baking dishes and keep one hot while serving the other.

Taco Tip

QUICK FIESTA DIP

makes: 1½ cups hands-on time: 3 min. total time: 8 min.

Talk about easy! With 3 ingredients and 8 minutes, you can make a fun and flavorful hot dip!

1½ cups thick-and-chunky mild salsa

1 (7-oz.) sweet whole kernel corn

1 cup (4 oz.) shredded colby or Cheddar cheese

1. Pour salsa into a 9-inch glass pie plate; stir in corn. Cover with plastic wrap; fold back a small section of wrap to allow steam to escape. Microwave at HIGH 2 minutes or until bubbly.

2. Sprinkle cheese over salsa; cover with plastic wrap. Let stand 5 minutes or until cheese is melted.

Use preshredded cheese from the dairy aisle. You can even shred cheese ahead and freeze it in 1-cup portions to have on hand when you need it.

SPEED It Up!

SPICY QUESO AND SAUSAGE DIP

makes: 30 servings   hands-on time: 20 min.   total time: 20 min.

1   lb. package ground pork sausage

2   (1-lb.) containers refrigerated spicy queso dip

1   (10-oz.) package frozen chopped spinach, thawed and drained

1   (15-oz.) can black beans, drained and rinsed

1   (10-oz.) can diced tomatoes and green chiles

Tortilla chips

1. Cook sausage in a large skillet over medium-high heat, stirring often, 8 to 10 minutes, until meat crumbles and is no longer pink; drain.

2. Meanwhile, heat queso dip in 2-qt. microwave-safe glass bowl according to package directions. Stir in sausage, spinach, and beans.

3. Drain tomatoes, reserving juice. Stir tomatoes and green chiles into dip. Stir in enough reserved juice (about 2 to 3 Tbsp.) to make dip spreadable. Reheat as needed. Serve warm with tortilla chips.

LAYERED NACHO DIP

makes: 8 cups hands-on time: 5 min. total time: 5 min.

With plenty of veggies, sour cream, and cheese, this meatless appetizer is sure to please any crowd.

1 (16-oz.) can refried beans

2 tsp. taco seasoning mix

1 (6-oz.) package refrigerated guacamole

1 (8-oz.) container sour cream

1 (4.25-oz.) can chopped black olives, drained

2 large tomatoes, diced

1 small onion, diced

1 (4.5-oz.) can chopped green chiles, drained

1½ cups (6 oz.) shredded Monterey Jack cheese

Corn chips or tortillas

1. Stir together beans and seasoning mix; spread mixture into an 11- x 7-inch baking dish. Spread guacamole and sour cream evenly over bean mixture. Sprinkle with olives and next 4 ingredients. Serve with corn chips or tortillas.

This dip can be made ahead and chilled up to 4 hours.

Taco Tip

TEXAS CAVIAR RICE AND BEANS

makes: 4 to 6 servings hands-on time: 20 min. total time: 45 min., including vinaigrette

1 (15.8-oz.) can black-eyed peas, drained and rinsed

1 (15-oz.) can black beans, drained and rinsed

⅓ cup finely chopped roasted red bell peppers

¼ cup finely chopped poblano pepper

Texas Vinaigrette, divided

2 (8.8-oz.) pouches fully cooked basmati rice

1¼ cups halved grape tomatoes

1 cup (4 oz.) shredded pepper Jack cheese

¾ cup loosely packed fresh cilantro leaves

⅔ cup thinly sliced celery

⅓ cup thinly sliced green onions

Tortilla chips

Garnish: sliced pickled jalapeño peppers

1. Stir together first 4 ingredients and ¼ cup Texas Vinaigrette in a microwave-safe glass bowl; let stand 20 minutes, stirring occasionally. Microwave at HIGH 2 minutes or until thoroughly heated, stirring at 30-second intervals.

2. Heat rice according to package directions; fluff with a fork. Divide bean mixture, rice, tomatoes, and next 4 ingredients among 4 to 6 individual plates. Serve with tortilla chips and remaining vinaigrette.

TEXAS VINAIGRETTE

makes: about 1 cup
hands-on time: 8 min.
total time: 8 min.

½ cup olive oil

¼ cup fresh lime juice

2 Tbsp. chopped fresh cilantro

1 Tbsp. hot sauce

1 garlic clove, minced

½ tsp. chili powder

½ tsp. ground cumin

Kosher salt

Black pepper

1. Whisk together first 7 ingredients. Add salt and pepper to taste.

PARTY PERFECT!

BEEF AND BLACK BEAN TACO CUPS

makes: 18 servings   hands-on time: 25 min. total time: 55 min.

These little cups are easy to pick up for a snack or an appetizer. You can also mix up the seasoned beef, black beans, and cheese blend and use it as a taco filling.

3   (8-oz.) cans refrigerated crescent rolls

¾   lb. lean ground beef

2   Tbsp. taco seasoning mix

1   (15-oz.) can black beans, drained and rinsed

1¼   cups (5 oz.) shredded Mexican four-cheese blend

1½   cups shredded iceberg lettuce

1   cup sour cream

1   cup salsa

1. Preheat oven to 375°.

2. Unroll crescent roll dough into 3 large rectangles; press each into a 12- x 8-inch rectangle, firmly pressing perforations to seal. Cut each rectangle into 6 (4-inch) squares. Gently press squares into 18 ungreased cups of 2 (12-cup) muffin pans.

3. Brown beef in a large skillet over medium-high heat, stirring occasionally, 5 to 7 minutes or until thoroughly cooked; drain. Mix beef, taco seasoning, and beans in a medium bowl. Divide evenly among dough cups. Sprinkle with cheese blend.

4. Bake at 375° for 18 to 22 minutes or until edges are golden brown. Cool 5 minutes. Run knife around edge of muffin cups to loosen. Remove from pan. Top with lettuce, sour cream, and salsa. Serve warm.

CHIPOTLE SHRIMP COCKTAIL

makes: 8 servings   hands-on time: 20 min.   total time: 12 hours, 20 min.

Chopped chipotle peppers in adobo sauce add a bit of zing to Chipotle Shrimp Cocktail.

- 1 **large red onion**
- 1 **medium-size red bell pepper**
- 1 **medium-size yellow bell pepper**
- 2 **lb. peeled, deveined, large cooked shrimp with tails**
- 1 **cup ketchup**
- ½ **cup chopped fresh cilantro**
- ½ **cup fresh lime juice**
- 3 **Tbsp. orange zest**
- ½ **cup fresh orange juice**
- 2 **to 3 canned chipotle peppers in adobo sauce, chopped**

1. Cut onion and bell peppers into thin strips; layer with shrimp in a large zip-top plastic freezer bag.

2. Whisk together ketchup and remaining ingredients; pour over shrimp mixture. Seal and chill 12 to 24 hours, turning bag occasionally. Serve using a slotted spoon.

TEX-MEX SHRIMP COCKTAIL

makes: 4 to 6 servings hands-on time: 15 min. total time: 4 hours, 15 min.

¼ cup hot red jalapeño pepper jelly

1 Tbsp. lime zest

¼ cup fresh lime juice

1 lb. peeled, large cooked shrimp (21/25 count)

1 cup diced mango

½ cup diced red bell pepper

¼ cup chopped fresh cilantro

1 small avocado, diced

Garnishes: lime slices, fresh cilantro sprigs

1. Whisk together first 3 ingredients. Pour into a large zip-top plastic freezer bag; add shrimp and next 3 ingredients, turning to coat. Seal and chill 4 hours, turning occasionally. Add avocado. Serve immediately.

Kids can chop cilantro using blunt-ended kitchen shears. Just put the cilantro in a bowl and let them snip it into smaller pieces.

Little Helpers

HOT & SPICY!

TOMATILLO-JALAPEÑO NACHOS

makes: 6 servings hands-on time: 15 min. total time: 30 min.

- **6 cups lime-flavored tortilla chips (from 13.5-oz. bag)**
- **1 cup (4 oz.) shredded sharp Cheddar cheese**
- **1 cup (4 oz.) shredded pepper Jack cheese**
- **1 (7-oz.) package refrigerated guacamole (from 14-oz. package)**
- **1 cup green tomatillo salsa**
- **1 jalapeño pepper, seeded and very thinly sliced**
- **2 Tbsp. chopped fresh cilantro**

1. Preheat oven to 400°. Spread tortilla chips on ungreased 18- x 13-inch baking sheet, overlapping slightly. Sprinkle with Cheddar cheese and pepper Jack cheese. Bake 10 to 12 minutes or until cheese melts.

2. Cut off small corner of guacamole bag; squeeze bag to drizzle guacamole over cheese and chips. Top with salsa; sprinkle with jalapeño and cilantro.

Note: We tested with Tostitos Hint of Lime tortilla chips and Wholly Guacamole.

Make these nachos in the microwave by assembling chips and cheese on a glass plate, microwaving at HIGH for 1 to 2 minutes, and then topping with remaining ingredients.

SPEED IT UP!

PORK CARNITA NACHOS

makes: 4 servings hands-on time: 10 min. total time: 6 hours, 10 min.

1 **onion, sliced**

2 **Tbsp. chopped canned chipotle peppers in adobo sauce or 2 fresh jalapeño peppers, seeded and sliced**

2 **to 3 lb. boned pork butt or shoulder**

4 **garlic cloves, slivered**

1 **Tbsp. vegetable oil**

Tortilla chips

Toppings: sliced jalapeño peppers, shredded Monterey Jack cheese, salsa verde, fresh salsa

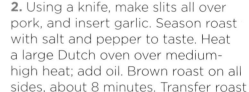

This slow-cooked pork mixture tastes great served as tacos in flour and corn tortillas.

1. Combine onion, chipotle peppers, and ¼ cup water in a 5-qt. slow cooker.

2. Using a knife, make slits all over pork, and insert garlic. Season roast with salt and pepper to taste. Heat a large Dutch oven over medium-high heat; add oil. Brown roast on all sides, about 8 minutes. Transfer roast to slow cooker. Pour ½ cup water into pan, stirring over low heat, using a wooden spoon to loosen browned particles from bottom of Dutch oven. Pour liquid into slow cooker. Cover and cook on HIGH for 6 hours.

3. Remove roast from slow cooker; let cool. Shred pork, using two forks. Return pulled pork to slow cooker, stirring to combine. Serve pork over tortilla chips with desired toppings.

STUFFED MINI PEPPERS

makes: 18 servings hands-on time: 10 min. total time: 35 min.

1   (1-lb.) bag mini sweet bell peppers (about 18 peppers)

1   (8-oz.) package cream cheese, softened

1   cup (4 oz.) shredded sharp Cheddar cheese

6   slices bacon, crisply cooked and crumbled (½ cup)

⅓   cup chopped green onions

2   Tbsp. chopped fresh cilantro

⅛   tsp. ground red pepper

1. Preheat oven to 425°. Place bell peppers on ungreased baking sheet. Bake for 8 minutes. Cool 5 minutes. Cut lengthwise slit in each pepper; discard seeds.

2. Mix remaining ingredients in a medium bowl. Spoon mixture evenly into peppers. Bake at 425° for 8 to 10 minutes or until lightly browned and cheese melts. Serve warm.

Taco Tip

Look for mini peppers in the produce section. If packaged in 8-oz. bags or 1-pt. plastic containers, you'll need 2 packages. The number of servings may vary due to the number of mini peppers in each package.

LIGHT & REFRESHING!

WATERMELON AGUA FRESCAS

makes: 5 cups hands-on time: 10 min. total time: 10 min.

This refreshing juice is perfect for a hot day at the beach, a picnic, or a porch sipper—no need to wait for Taco Night!

4   **cups cubed seedless watermelon, cantaloupe, or honeydew melon**

¼   **cup sugar**

2   **cups cold water**

1. Process watermelon, cantaloupe, or honeydew melon and sugar in a blender until smooth, stopping to scrape down sides as needed.

2. Pour mixture through a fine wire-mesh strainer into a pitcher, discarding solids. Stir in 2 cups cold water. Cover and chill until ready to serve. Serve over ice.

LITTLE HELPERS

This recipe is so easy, even the kids can master it. Plus, they will be more apt to drink this fruit-packed beverage!

HOMEMADE LIMEADE

makes: 8 cups hands-on time: 10 min. total time: 8 hours, 10 min.

Nothing is more refreshing than an ice-cold glass of limeade, the perfect accompaniment to spicy Tex-Mex food.

1½	cups sugar	1½	cups fresh lime juice
½	cup boiling water	5	cups cold water
2	tsp. grated lime zest		Garnish: lime slices

1. Stir together sugar and ½ cup boiling water until sugar dissolves. Stir in lime zest, lime juice, and 5 cups cold water. Chill 8 hours.

COCOA-COCONUT COFFEE COOLER

makes: about 8 cups hands-on time: 15 min. total time: 1 hour, 15 min.

This is almost a dessert! Stir in 1 cup dark rum or bourbon for an even more festive sipper.

4	cups strong brewed hot chicory coffee	1	(13.5-oz.) can coconut milk
½	cup sugar	2	tsp. vanilla extract
¼	cup unsweetened cocoa	¼	tsp. coconut extract
2	cups half-and-half		

1. Whisk together hot coffee, sugar, and cocoa in a large pitcher until cocoa and sugar dissolve. Whisk in half-and-half, coconut milk, vanilla, and coconut extract until blended. Chill 1 to 24 hours. Stir just before serving over ice.

CLASSIC MARGARITA

makes: 1 serving hands-on time: 5 min. total time: 5 min.

The only margarita recipe you'll need, this easy cocktail is a simple mix of shaken fresh lime juice, orange liqueur, tequila, and powdered sugar.

Fresh lime wedge (optional)

Margarita salt (optional)

Ice

⅓ cup fresh lime juice

3 Tbsp. orange liqueur

2 Tbsp. tequila

⅓ to ½ cup powdered sugar

Garnish: lime slice

For an even quicker version, you can substitute ⅓ cup thawed frozen limeade concentrate for fresh lime juice. Omit powdered sugar, and proceed with recipe as directed.

SPEED IT UP!

1. Rub rim of a chilled margarita glass with lime wedge, and dip rim in salt to coat, if desired.

2. Fill cocktail shaker half full with ice. Add lime juice, orange liqueur, tequila, and powdered sugar; cover with lid, and shake until thoroughly chilled. Strain into prepared glass.

Note: We tested with Cointreau orange liqueur.

Frozen Margarita: Combine lime juice, liqueur, tequila, and powdered sugar in a small pitcher or measuring cup; stir until powdered sugar dissolves. Pour into a zip-top plastic freezer bag. Seal and freeze 8 hours. Let stand 5 minutes at room temperature before serving. Pour into prepared glass. Makes 1 serving.

Frozen Strawberry Margaritas: Process lime juice, liqueur, tequila, powdered sugar, 1 cup fresh or frozen strawberries, and 1 cup crushed ice in a blender until slushy. Rub rim of 2 chilled margarita glasses with lime wedge, and dip rim in red decorator sugar to coat, if desired. Serve immediately in prepared glasses. Makes 2 servings.

CRANBERRY-LIME MARGARITAS

makes: 26 servings   hands-on time: 10 min.   total time: 30 min.

1   cup sugar

1   cup fresh lime juice

1½   cups tequila

½   cup orange liqueur

1   (64-oz.) bottle cranberry juice cocktail (8 cups)

Lime wedges

Coarse (kosher or sea) salt

Crushed ice

Garnish: Additional lime wedges

1. Heat sugar and 1 cup water in a 1-qt. saucepan over medium heat until sugar dissolves. Remove pan from heat. Pour into large heatproof pitcher. Cover; refrigerate 20 minutes.

2. Add lime juice, tequila, orange liqueur, and cranberry juice cocktail to sugar syrup in pitcher; mix well. Refrigerate until serving time.

3. Rub rims of margarita or lowball glasses with lime wedges, and dip rims in salt to coat. Fill glasses with crushed ice; pour margarita mixture over ice.

STRAWBERRY MARGARITA SPRITZERS

makes: about 8 cups hands-on time: 10 min. total time: 10 min.

1   (10-oz.) package frozen whole strawberries, thawed

1   (10-oz.) can frozen strawberry daiquiri mix, thawed

1   cup tequila

¼   cup orange liqueur

2   Tbsp. fresh lime juice

1   (1-liter) bottle club soda, chilled

Garnish: halved fresh strawberries

1. Pulse first 5 ingredients in a blender until smooth. Pour into a pitcher, and stir in club soda just before serving. Serve over ice.

Note: We tested with Triple Sec orange liqueur.

BEER'GARITAS

makes: about 6 cups hands-on time: 5 min. total time: 5 min.

1   (12-oz.) container limeade concentrate, thawed

1½ cups tequila

2   (12-oz.) bottles beer

Crushed ice

Garnish: lime wedges

1. Stir together first 3 ingredients in a large pitcher until blended. Serve immediately over crushed ice.

Take Your Pick!

Tacos Deliciosos

Try these great tacos—
from chicken and beef to vegetarian and seafood.

TEX-MEX VEGETARIAN FAJITAS

makes: 8 servings hands-on time: 40 min. total time: 40 min.

1   (14-oz.) package extra-firm tofu, drained and cut crosswise into ½-inch-thick pieces

1   tsp. ground cumin

1   tsp. chili powder

7   tsp. vegetable oil, divided

½   sweet onion, thinly sliced

1   red bell pepper, cut into thin strips

½   cup chunky salsa

2   tsp. cider vinegar

1   tsp. table salt

8   (6-inch) fajita-size flour tortillas, warmed

Toppings: shredded lettuce, shredded cheese, guacamole, sour cream

1. Sprinkle tofu with cumin and chili powder; gently toss to coat all sides.

2. Cook half of tofu in 3 tsp. hot oil in a large nonstick skillet over medium heat 5 minutes on each side. Remove tofu, and keep warm. Repeat procedure with 3 tsp. oil and remaining tofu.

3. Sauté sliced onion and bell pepper in remaining 1 tsp. hot oil in skillet over medium-high heat 2 minutes or until tender. Stir in salsa, vinegar, and salt; cook 2 minutes. Pour mixture over tofu. Serve with warm tortillas and desired toppings.

Note: We tested with Nasoya Organic Extra Firm Tofu and Pace Chunky Salsa.

For chicken fajitas, substitute 1 lb. chopped cooked chicken breast in place of the tofu, and cook for 7 minutes, stirring often.

Taco Tip

BUTTERMILK FRIED OKRA TACOS

makes: 8 servings hands-on time: 40 min. total time: 40 min., including salsa

A sprinkling of sugar in the cornmeal coating caramelizes as the okra cooks, creating a crisp, golden crust.

1   lb. fresh okra, cut into ½-inch-thick slices

¾   cup buttermilk

1½ cups self-rising white cornmeal mix

1   tsp. table salt

1   tsp. sugar

¼   tsp. ground red pepper

Vegetable oil

16 (8-inch) soft taco-size corn or flour tortillas

Fresh Tomato Salsa

Toppings: shredded lettuce, shredded pepper Jack cheese, guacamole, sour cream

1. Stir together okra and buttermilk in a large bowl. Stir together cornmeal mix and next 3 ingredients in a separate large bowl. Remove okra from buttermilk, in batches, using a slotted spoon. Dredge in cornmeal mixture, and place in a wire-mesh strainer. Shake off excess.

2. Pour oil to depth of 1 inch into a large, deep cast-iron skillet or Dutch oven; heat to 375°. Fry okra, in batches, 4 minutes or until golden, turning once. Drain on paper towels.

3. Fill warm tortillas with hot fried okra and Fresh Tomato Salsa. Serve with desired toppings.

FRESH TOMATO SALSA

makes: 8 servings
hands-on time: 40 min.
total time: 40 min.

3   cups seeded and diced tomatoes

1   large avocado, diced

1   small green bell pepper, diced

1   (2.25-oz.) can sliced black olives, drained

½   cup chopped green onions

⅓   cup chopped fresh cilantro

1½ tsp. balsamic vinegar

½   tsp. seasoned salt

1. Stir together all ingredients. Season with table salt to taste.

VEGETARIAN!

MEXICALI MEATLESS TOSTADAS

makes: 6 servings   hands-on time: 10 min.   total time: 15 min.

1   **(12-oz.) package frozen meatless burger crumbles**

3   **tsp. taco seasoning**

12 **tostada shells**

1   **(8.5-oz.) package ready-to-serve whole grain Santa Fe rice**

1   **(16-oz.) can refried beans**

1   **(8-oz.) package shredded Mexican four-cheese blend**

Topping: pico de gallo

1. Preheat oven to 425°. Prepare crumbles according to package directions. Stir taco seasoning into hot crumble mixture. Prepare tostada shells and rice according to package directions.

2. Layer refried beans, crumble mixture, and rice on tostada shells. Sprinkle with cheese. Bake at 425° for 5 to 6 minutes or until cheese melts. Serve with pico de gallo.

Note: We tested with MorningStar Farms® Meal Starters Grillers® Recipe Crumbles™.

Let the kids layer up tostada shells with refried beans, crumble mixture, rice, and cheese. Adults can bake them and serve.

Little Helpers

BREAKFAST IN A TACO!

MIGAS TACOS

makes: 2 servings hands-on time: 10 min. total time: 15 min.

These Tex-Mex breakfast tacos filled with cheesy scrambled eggs are a great breakfast-for-dinner dish.

⅓ **cup lightly crushed tortilla chips**

¼ **cup chopped onion**

¼ **cup diced tomatoes**

2 **Tbsp. chopped jalapeño peppers**

1 **tsp. vegetable oil**

2 **large eggs, lightly beaten**

2 **(8-inch) soft taco-size flour tortillas, warmed**

½ **cup (2 oz.) shredded Mexican four-cheese blend**

1. Sauté first 4 ingredients in hot oil in a medium-size nonstick skillet over medium heat 3 to 4 minutes or just until onion is translucent.

2. Whisk together eggs with salt and pepper to taste. Add to skillet, and cook, without stirring, 1 to 2 minutes or until eggs begin to set on bottom. Gently draw cooked edges away from sides of pan to form large pieces. Cook, stirring occasionally, 2 minutes or until eggs are thickened and moist. (Do not over stir.)

3. Spoon egg mixture into warm tortillas, and sprinkle with cheese; serve immediately.

SOUTHWEST SHRIMP TACOS

makes: 8 servings   hands-on time: 34 min.   total time: 34 min.

Serve with hot sauce, Mexican crema or regular sour cream, and chopped radishes.

- 10 to 12 (10-inch) wooden skewers
- 2 lb. unpeeled, large raw shrimp (21/25 count)
- Vegetable cooking spray
- 2 Tbsp. hot sauce
- 1 Tbsp. olive oil
- 1½ tsp. ancho chile powder
- 1½ tsp. ground cumin
- ¾ tsp. table salt
- 16 to 20 (8-inch) soft taco-size corn or flour tortillas
- 3 cups shredded cabbage
- 1 cup grated carrots
- Lime wedges

1. Soak skewers in water 20 minutes.

2. Meanwhile, peel shrimp; devein, if desired. Coat cold cooking grate of grill with cooking spray, and place on grill. Preheat grill to 350° to 400° (medium-high) heat.

3. Toss shrimp with hot sauce and next 4 ingredients. Thread shrimp onto skewers. Grill shrimp, covered with grill lid, 1 to 2 minutes on each side or just until shrimp turn pink. Grill tortillas 1 minute on each side or until warmed.

4. Combine cabbage and carrots. Remove shrimp from skewers just before serving. Serve shrimp in warm tortillas with cabbage mixture and lime wedges.

Let the store do the work for you by buying large peeled and deveined shrimp in the seafood section.

SPEED IT UP!

GREAT
GRILLED
FLAVOR!

CITRUS SHRIMP TACOS

makes: 6 to 8 servings   hands-on time: 25 min.   total time: 41 min., including sauce

2   lb. unpeeled, large raw shrimp

20 (12-inch) skewers

2   Tbsp. Southwest seasoning

3   garlic cloves, minced

⅓   cup lime juice

3   Tbsp. lemon juice

16 (8-inch) soft taco-size flour tortillas, warmed

1   head iceberg lettuce, finely shredded

1   head radicchio, finely shredded

Southwest Cream Sauce

Grilled Corn Salsa (page 15)

Garnish: fresh cilantro leaves

1. Peel shrimp; devein, if desired. Thread shrimp onto skewers.

2. Preheat grill to 350° to 400° (medium-high) heat. Combine Southwest seasoning and garlic in a long shallow dish; add lime juice, lemon juice, and shrimp, turning to coat. Cover and chill 10 minutes. Remove shrimp from marinade, discarding marinade.

3. Grill shrimp, without grill lid, 2 to 3 minutes on each side or just until shrimp turn pink. Remove shrimp from skewers. Serve in warm tortillas with lettuce, radicchio, Southwest Cream Sauce, and Grilled Corn Salsa.

Note: We tested with Emeril's Southwest Seasoning.

SOUTHWEST CREAM SAUCE

makes: about 2 cups
hands-on time: 8 min.
total time: 8 min.

1   (16-oz.) container sour cream

1   garlic clove, minced

2   Tbsp. finely chopped red onion

1   tsp. chili powder

½   tsp. ground cumin

½   tsp. ground red pepper

¼   tsp. table salt

2   Tbsp. chopped fresh cilantro

2   Tbsp. fresh lime juice

1. Whisk together first 7 ingredients. Whisk in cilantro and lime juice until smooth. Cover and chill until ready to serve.

SPICY FISH TACOS
WITH MANGO SALSA AND GUACAMOLE

makes: 4 to 6 servings hands-on time: 20 min. total time: 25 min., including salsa

6   (6-oz.) flounder fillets
1   lime
2   Tbsp. chili powder
2   tsp. table salt
2   teaspoons ground cumin
½   teaspoon ground red pepper
1½ cups plain yellow cornmeal
Vegetable oil

4   to 6 flour or corn tortillas
Mango Salsa
Classic Guacamole (page 9)
Toppings: shredded iceberg lettuce, chopped tomato
Garnishes: lime wedges, fresh cilantro sprigs

MANGO SALSA

makes: 1 cup
hands-on time: 10 min.
total time: 10 min.

1   mango, chopped
1   jalapeño pepper, seeded and finely chopped
1   garlic clove, minced
1   Tbsp. fresh lime juice
1   Tbsp. finely chopped red onion
1   Tbsp. chopped fresh cilantro
¼   tsp. table salt

1. Stir together all ingredients. Cover and chill until ready to serve.

1. Place fish in a shallow dish. Squeeze juice of 1 lime over fillets.

2. Combine chili powder and next 3 ingredients. Sprinkle 1½ Tbsp. seasoning mixture evenly over fish, coating both sides of fillets. Reserve remaining seasoning mixture.

3. Combine cornmeal and reserved seasoning mixture in a shallow dish. Dredge fish fillets in cornmeal mixture, shaking off excess.

4. Pour oil to a depth of 1½ inches in a Dutch oven; heat to 350°. Fry fillets, in batches, 2 to 3 minutes or until golden brown. Drain fillets on wire racks over paper towels.

5. Break each fillet into chunks, using a fork. Place fish in warmed tortillas, and serve with Mango Salsa, Classic Guacamole, and desired toppings.

POBLANO FISH TACOS

makes: 6 servings hands-on time: 22 min. total time: 40 min.

1   large poblano pepper

½   English cucumber, coarsely chopped

1   cup grape tomatoes, quartered

2   Tbsp. chopped red onion

1   garlic clove, minced

½   tsp. table salt

3   Tbsp. fresh lime juice, divided

4   Tbsp. olive oil, divided

1   Tbsp. mango-lime seafood seasoning

1½ lb. grouper or other firm white fish fillets

12 (6-inch) fajita-size corn tortillas, warmed

Lime wedges

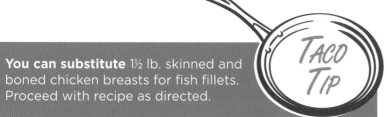

You can substitute 1½ lb. skinned and boned chicken breasts for fish fillets. Proceed with recipe as directed.

1. Preheat grill to 350° to 400° (medium-high) heat. Grill pepper, covered with grill lid, 3 to 4 minutes or until pepper looks blistered, turning once. Place pepper in a large zip-top plastic freezer bag; seal and let stand 10 minutes to loosen skins. Peel pepper; remove and discard seeds. Coarsely chop.

2. Combine pepper, cucumber, next 4 ingredients, 2 Tbsp. lime juice and 2 Tbsp. olive oil in a bowl.

3. Whisk together seafood seasoning and remaining 1 Tbsp. lime juice and 2 Tbsp. olive oil in a large shallow dish or zip-top plastic freezer bag; add fish, turning to coat. Cover or seal, and chill 5 minutes, turning once. Remove fish from marinade, discarding marinade.

4. Grill fish, covered with grill lid, 3 to 4 minutes on each side or just until fish begins to flake when poked with the tip of a sharp knife and is opaque in center. Cool 5 minutes. Flake fish into bite-size pieces.

5. Serve fish and salsa in warm tortillas with lime wedges.

Note: We tested with Weber® Mango Lime Seafood Seasoning.

CRISPY FISH TACOS

makes: 10 servings hands-on time: 15 min. total time: 30 min., including crema

1 **(18.2-oz.) package frozen beer-battered fish fillets**

2 **cups packed angel hair coleslaw (from 10-oz. bag)**

⅓ **cup chopped fresh cilantro**

10 **(6-inch) soft corn tortillas, heated as directed on package**

1 **large ripe mango, peeled and chopped**

Jalapeño-Lime Crema

Lime wedges

1. Preheat oven to 425°F.

2. Bake fish according to package directions. Cool slightly.

3. Toss coleslaw and cilantro together in a medium bowl. Place 1 fish fillet on each tortilla; top evenly with coleslaw mixture and mango. Drizzle with Jalapeño-Lime Crema. Squeeze lime over each taco before serving.

JALAPEÑO-LIME CREMA

makes: about 1 cup
hands-on time: 5 min.
total time: 5 min.

½ **cup sour cream**

⅓ **cup whipping cream**

2 **tsp. lime zest**

¼ **tsp. table salt**

1 **large jalapeño pepper, seeded and finely chopped**

1. Mix all ingredients in a small bowl. Refrigerate until ready to serve.

GRILLED CHICKEN TACOS

makes: 4 to 6 servings   hands-on time: 20 min.   total time: 32 min.

3   Tbsp. olive oil

2   Tbsp. lime juice

4   tsp. Montreal chicken seasoning

1½ lb. chicken breast tenders

1   (8-oz.) container refrigerated fresh salsa

1   large mango, peeled and chopped

¼   cup chopped fresh cilantro

2   tsp. chipotle hot sauce

6   (6-inch) fajita-size flour tortillas, warmed

Toppings: crumbled queso fresco (fresh Mexican cheese), shredded romaine lettuce

1. Preheat grill to 300° to 350° (medium) heat. Combine first 3 ingredients in a zip-top plastic freezer bag; add chicken, turning to coat. Seal and chill 10 minutes, turning once.

2. Meanwhile, combine salsa and next 3 ingredients. Cover and chill until ready to serve.

3. Remove chicken from marinade, discarding marinade. Grill chicken, covered with grill lid, 6 minutes on each side or until done. Serve in flour tortillas with mango salsa and desired toppings.

Note: We tested with McCormick's Grill Mates® Montreal Chicken Seasoning.

SHREDDED CHICKEN TACOS

makes: 4 servings hands-on time: 17 min. total time: 25 min.

2   ears fresh corn, husks removed

1   (12-oz.) package baby heirloom tomatoes

½   tsp. black pepper

¼   tsp. table salt

2   cups shredded skinless, boneless rotisserie chicken breast

8   (6-inch) fajita-size flour tortillas, warmed

1   avocado, peeled and sliced

Lime wedges

1. Preheat broiler.

2. Place corn on a jelly-roll pan; broil 18 minutes or until charred on all sides, rotating every 6 minutes. Cut kernels from corn; place kernels in a medium bowl. Cut tomatoes into quarters. Add tomatoes to corn, and sprinkle corn mixture with pepper and salt.

3. Divide chicken evenly among warm tortillas; top each with ¼ cup corn mixture and avocado slices. Serve with lime wedges.

Taco Tip

Top with crumbled queso fresco (fresh Mexican cheese) for a south-of-the-border flair.

SURPRISINGLY EASY!

EASY BARBECUE TOSTADAS

makes: 10 servings hands-on time: 10 min. total time: 30 min., including slaw

½ cup sour cream

1 chipotle pepper in adobo sauce, minced

Pinch of table salt

1 Tbsp. mole sauce

¼ cup hot water

1 cup barbecue sauce

1 Tbsp. lime juice

1 Tbsp. chopped fresh cilantro

10 tostada shells

1 (16-oz.) can refried beans

2 lb. shredded barbecued pork or chicken without sauce

Jicama Slaw

1. Stir together sour cream, chipotle pepper, and salt. Refrigerate until ready to use.

2. Dissolve mole sauce in ¼ cup hot water, whisking until smooth. Whisk in barbecue sauce, lime juice, and cilantro.

3. Spread tostada shells with refried beans. Top with barbecued pork or chicken, mole barbecue sauce, chipotle sour cream, and Jicama Slaw. Serve immediately.

Pick up shredded pork or chicken from your favorite barbecue joint.

JICAMA SLAW

makes: about 4½ cups
hands-on time: 10 min.
total time: 10 min.

2 cups shredded red cabbage

2 cups thinly sliced jimaca (about ½ medium jicama)

¼ cup thinly sliced red onion

¼ cup chopped fresh cilantro

1 Tbsp. olive oil

1 Tbsp. fresh lime juice

½ tsp. table salt

½ tsp. sugar

1. Toss together all ingredients. Serve immediately or cover and chill up to 1 hour.

GRILLED PORK TACOS

makes: 6 servings   hands-on time: 15 min.   total time: 1 hour, 5 min., including slaw

Here's a delicious (and healthy!) change of pace from the usual ground beef tacos.

- **6   (1-inch-thick) boneless pork chops**
- **Cilantro Slaw**
- **2   Tbsp. olive oil**
- **1   tsp. kosher salt**
- **½   tsp. freshly ground pepper**
- **12   (6-inch) fajita-size flour tortillas, warmed**
- **Lime wedges**

1. Let pork stand at room temperature 30 to 40 minutes. Meanwhile, prepare Cilantro Slaw. Light 1 side of grill, heating to 350° to 400° (medium-high) heat; leave other side unlit. Brush pork with olive oil, and sprinkle with salt and pepper.

2. Grill pork over lit side of grill, covered with grill lid, 4 minutes on each side; transfer pork to unlit side, and grill, covered with grill lid, 10 minutes on each side or until a meat thermometer inserted into thickest portion registers 145°. Let stand 5 minutes. Thinly slice pork.

3. Place pork in warm tortillas; top with Cilantro Slaw. Serve with lime wedges.

CILANTRO SLAW

makes: about 6 cups
hands-on time: 10 min.
total time: 10 min.

- **½   small head napa cabbage, thinly sliced (about 4 cups)**
- **1   (8-oz.) can pineapple tidbits, drained**
- **⅓   cup thinly sliced green onions**
- **⅓   cup chopped radishes (about 2 large)**
- **¼   cup thinly sliced sweet onion**
- **¼   cup shredded carrot**
- **¼   cup finely chopped fresh cilantro**
- **2   Tbsp. Champagne vinegar**
- **1   Tbsp. olive oil**

1. Toss together all ingredients. Serve immediately or cover and chill up to 1 hour.

SWEET 'N' SPICY BRAISED PORK TACOS

makes: 8 to 10 servings   hands-on time: 10 min.   total time: 10 hours, 10 min.

Enjoy this slow-cooked Latin American dish atop black beans and rice inside flour tortillas. Serve with lime wedges.

- **3   lb. boneless pork shoulder roast (Boston butt)**
- **½   tsp. table salt**
- **½   tsp. freshly ground pepper**
- **1   Tbsp. vegetable oil**
- **2   (14½-oz.) cans diced tomatoes with garlic and onion**
- **1   medium-size sweet onion, chopped**
- **1   to 2 chipotle peppers in adobo sauce, chopped**
- **2   Tbsp. cider vinegar**
- **2   Tbsp. dark brown sugar**
- **¼   tsp. ground cumin**
- **6   cups cooked white rice**
- **1   (15-oz.) can black beans**
- **16   to 20 (6-inch) fajita-size flour tortillas, warmed**
- **Garnishes: fresh cilantro sprigs, lime wedges**

1. Sprinkle pork with salt and pepper. Cook pork in hot oil in a large skillet over medium-high heat 2 to 3 minutes on all sides or until pork is browned. Stir together tomatoes and next 5 ingredients in a 5-qt. slow cooker. Add pork, turning to coat.

2. Cover and cook on LOW 10 hours or until pork is fork-tender. Transfer pork to a cutting board, and let stand 10 minutes.

3. Shred pork with 2 forks. Return shredded pork to slow cooker, and stir until blended. Season with salt and pepper to taste, if desired. Serve immediately with a slotted spoon over rice and black beans in tortillas.

TACOS AL PASTOR

makes: 6 tacos hands-on time: 15 min. total time: 4 hours, 25 min.

Tacos Al Pastor is a Mexican dish featuring a pork and pineapple mixture. These tacos are generally served on soft tortillas and include cilantro, onions, lime juice, pineapple, and salsa.

1   lb. pork tenderloin, cut into ½-inch cubes

1   (8-oz.) can pineapple tidbits in juice, drained

1   medium onion, chopped

¼   cup chopped fresh cilantro

1   Tbsp. Mexican-style chili powder

1   tsp. ground cumin

1   tsp. dried oregano

1   tsp. pepper

1   tsp. chopped garlic

¾   tsp. table salt

1   Tbsp. canola oil

6   (8-inch) soft taco-size corn or flour tortillas, warmed

Toppings: chopped radishes, fresh cilantro leaves, crumbled queso fresco (fresh Mexican cheese), chopped onions, chopped jalapeño pepper

1. Combine pork and next 9 ingredients in a large zip-top plastic freezer bag. Seal and chill 4 to 24 hours.

2. Cook pork mixture in hot oil in a large nonstick skillet over medium-high heat, stirring often, 10 minutes or until pork is done. Serve mixture with warm tortillas and desired toppings.

Spicy Chicken-Pineapple Tacos: Substitute 1 lb. skinned and boned chicken thighs, chopped, for pork tenderloin. Proceed with recipe as directed.

Pineapple acts as a natural tenderizer to the pork, resulting in flavorful, tender meat.

Taco Tip

Authentic & Flavorful!

PICADILLO TACOS

makes: 8 servings hands-on time: 15 min. total time: 30 min.

Lots of veggies combined with ground beef make for a hearty, nutritious dinner the whole family will love.

1	lb. ground round
1	Tbsp. vegetable oil
2	carrots, diced
1	small onion, diced
½	tsp. table salt
2	plum tomatoes, diced

1   to 2 canned chipotle peppers in adobo sauce, minced

8   (8-inch) soft taco-size corn or flour tortillas, warmed

Garnish: fresh cilantro sprigs

This meaty mixture is also great served over salad greens or wrapped in enchiladas and burritos.

1. Cook ground round in hot oil in a large skillet over medium-high heat, stirring often, 7 minutes or until meat crumbles and is no longer pink; drain.

2. Stir in carrots, onion, and salt; sauté 5 minutes. Add tomatoes and chipotle peppers, and cook, stirring occasionally, 3 to 4 minutes or until tomatoes begin to soften.

3. Serve mixture with warm tortillas.

Vegetarian Picadillo Tacos
Substitute 1 (12-oz.) package frozen meatless burger crumbles* for ground round. Proceed with recipe as directed, sautéing crumbles in hot oil 3 to 4 minutes.

*Note: We tested with MorningStar Farms® Meal Starters Grillers® Recipe Crumbles™.

SLOW-COOKER BEEF TACOS

makes: 8 servings   hands-on time: 15 min.   total time: 8 hours, 15 min.

2   lb. boneless beef chuck roast, cut into 1-inch cubes

1   tsp. table salt

1   Tbsp. vegetable oil

1   Tbsp. chili powder

1   (6-oz.) can tomato paste

2   cups beef broth

1   small white onion, sliced

1   (8-oz.) can tomato sauce

½   medium-size green bell pepper

1   tsp. ground cumin

½   tsp. black pepper

8   taco shells

Toppings: shredded Cheddar cheese, shredded lettuce, fresh salsa

1. Sprinkle beef with salt.

2. Cook beef in hot oil in a Dutch oven over medium-high heat 8 minutes or until browned on all sides. Remove beef, reserving drippings in Dutch oven. Add 1 Tbsp. chili powder to Dutch oven; cook, stirring constantly, 1 minute. Stir in tomato paste, and cook, stirring constantly, 2 minutes. Add beef broth, stirring to loosen particles from bottom of Dutch oven. Return beef to Dutch oven, and stir.

3. Place beef mixture in a 5-qt. slow cooker. Add onion and next 4 ingredients. Cook on LOW 8 hours or until beef is tender. Serve with taco shells and desired toppings.

Browning the beef before slow cooking adds color and enhances the flavor. This mixture is also great over baked potatoes with your favorite toppings.

A Taco Night Fave!

GLOBAL FLAVOR!

VIETNAMESE BARBECUE TACOS

makes: 8 servings hands-on time: 30 min. total time: 8 hours, 50 min., including dipping sauce

These tacos get a global vibe with ingredients such as ginger, sesame oil, and fish sauce.

3   beef strip steaks (about 2½ lb.)

¼   cup fish sauce

¼   cup rice wine vinegar

2   Tbsp. grated fresh ginger

3   garlic cloves, minced

2   Tbsp. sugar

2   Tbsp. honey

1   Tbsp. sesame oil

1   tsp. black pepper

½   medium-size red onion, sliced

8   (8-inch) soft taco-size flour tortillas, warmed

Vietnamese Dipping Sauce

Toppings: sliced red cabbage, matchstick carrots, sliced red onion, chopped fresh cilantro and mint, cucumber slices

1. Place steaks in a large zip-top plastic freezer bag. Whisk together fish sauce and next 7 ingredients. Stir in red onion, and pour mixture over steaks in freezer bag. Seal and chill 8 to 24 hours, turning once.

2. Preheat grill to 350° to 400° (medium-high) heat. Remove steaks from marinade, discarding marinade.

3. Grill steaks 7 to 8 minutes on each side or to desired degree of doneness, turning every 3 to 5 minutes. Cover loosely with aluminum foil, and let stand 10 minutes.

4. Cut steaks diagonally across the grain into thin strips, and serve in warm flour tortillas with Vietnamese Dipping Sauce and desired toppings.

VIETNAMESE DIPPING SAUCE

makes: about 1 cup
hands-on time: 5 min.
total time: 5 min.

¼   cup fish sauce

¼   cup rice vinegar

3   Tbsp. sugar

2   Tbsp. lime juice

2   garlic cloves, minced

1   serrano pepper, seeded and sliced

1. Stir together all ingredients and ½ cup water in a medium bowl. Store in an airtight container in refrigerator up to 1 week.

BEEF BRISKET SOFT TACOS

makes: 6 to 8 servings hands-on time: 15 min. total time: 6 hours, 15 min.

2 medium onions, thinly sliced

2 celery ribs, thinly sliced

2 garlic cloves, pressed

1 (2-lb.) beef brisket

2 tsp. table salt

1½ tsp. ground chipotle powder

1 cup coarsely chopped fresh cilantro

10 (8-inch) flour tortillas

Toppings: shredded Mexican four-cheese blend, sour cream, salsa, chopped fresh cilantro

Lime wedges

1. Place first 3 ingredients in a 6-qt. slow cooker.

2. Trim fat from brisket; cut brisket into 3-inch pieces. Rub brisket pieces with table salt and chipotle powder, and place on top of vegetables in slow cooker. Top with cilantro.

3. Cover and cook on HIGH 6 hours or until brisket pieces shred easily with a fork.

4. Remove brisket from slow cooker, and cool slightly. Shred into bite-size pieces with 2 forks; return to slow cooker and stir. Serve in flour tortillas with desired toppings and lime wedges.

Taco Tip

When shopping, select a brisket that is uniform in thickness to make shredding the meat easier.

GRILLED FLANK STEAK FAJITAS

makes: 4 servings   hands-on time: 30 min.   total time: 30 min.

1½ Tbsp. canola oil, divided

1 tsp. chili powder

1 tsp. ground cumin

1 tsp. table salt, divided

¾ tsp. freshly ground black pepper, divided

1 (1½-lb.) flank steak

1 (16-oz.) package frozen pepper stir-fry with onion

¼ cup chopped fresh cilantro

8 (6-inch) fajita-size flour tortillas, warmed

1 (7-oz.) package refrigerated guacamole

½ cup (2 oz.) crumbled queso fresco (fresh Mexican cheese)

1. Preheat grill to 350° to 400° (medium-high) heat. Stir together 1 Tbsp. oil, chili powder, cumin, ½ tsp. salt, and ½ tsp. black pepper; rub over steak.

2. Grill steak, covered with grill lid, 8 minutes on each side or to desired degree of doneness. Let stand 10 minutes.

3. Meanwhile, heat remaining ½ Tbsp. oil in a large skillet over medium-high heat. Add frozen vegetables, remaining ½ tsp. salt and ¼ tsp. black pepper; sauté 6 minutes. Stir in cilantro; sauté 2 minutes.

4. Cut steak diagonally across the grain into thin strips. Serve steak and vegetables with warm tortillas, guacamole, and cheese.

SPEED IT UP!

By using frozen bell pepper mix, you can make a quick and easy topping for these fajitas without any cutting or thawing required. Just toss the peppers in the skillet and sauté!

MEXICAN DINNERS

Make dinnertime a fiesta

with these enchiladas, quesadillas,
chimichangas, and more!

TACO SALAD

makes: 6 servings hands-on time: 25 min. total time: 25 min.

1½ lb. lean ground beef

1 (16-oz.) jar medium salsa

1 (16-oz.) can kidney beans, drained and rinsed

2 Tbsp. taco seasoning mix

2 avocados

½ cup sour cream

2 Tbsp. fresh cilantro

Bite-size tortilla chips

3 cups shredded lettuce (about ½ head)

Toppings: chopped tomato, finely chopped red onion, shredded cheese

1. Brown ground beef in a large nonstick skillet over medium-high heat, stirring often, 5 to 8 minutes or until meat crumbles and is no longer pink; drain and return to skillet. Stir in salsa, beans, and taco seasoning; bring to a boil. Reduce heat, and simmer, stirring occasionally, 10 minutes.

2. Peel and mash avocados; stir in sour cream and cilantro.

3. Place desired amount of tortilla chips on a serving platter, and top with shredded lettuce and beef mixture. Serve with avocado mixture and desired toppings.

Kids will have a blast mashing up the avocados in step 2.

LITTLE HELPERS

MEXICAN TOMATO SOUP

makes: 4 to 6 servings   hands-on time: 1 hour, 5 min.   total time: 1 hour, 40 min.

6   (6-inch) corn tortillas

2   Tbsp. canola oil, divided

2   medium tomatoes, cored and halved

1   onion, chopped

2   garlic cloves

1   (32-oz.) container reduced-sodium fat-free chicken broth

2   cups low-sodium tomato juice

1   bay leaf

¼   tsp. ground cumin

¼   tsp. ground coriander

¼   tsp. ground red pepper

1½ lb. skinned and boned chicken breasts, cut into ½-inch-wide strips

4   green onions (white part only), thinly sliced

½   cup fresh lime juice

¼   cup chopped fresh cilantro

½   cup (2 oz.) crumbled queso fresco (fresh Mexican cheese)

1   medium avocado, chopped

1. Preheat oven to 400°. Brush 1 side of tortillas with 1 Tbsp. oil; cut tortillas in half. Stack tortilla halves, and cut crosswise into ¼-inch-wide strips. Arrange strips in a single layer on a lightly greased baking sheet. Season with salt and pepper to taste. Bake 15 minutes or until golden, stirring halfway through. Cool.

2. Meanwhile, heat a nonstick skillet over high heat 2 minutes. Add tomato halves, and cook, turning occasionally, 10 minutes or until charred on all sides. (Tomatoes may stick.) Transfer to a food processor.

3. Sauté onion in remaining 1 Tbsp. hot oil in skillet over medium heat 3 to 5 minutes or until tender. Add garlic; sauté 2 minutes or until fragrant. Transfer onion mixture to food processor with tomatoes; process until smooth.

4. Cook tomato mixture in a Dutch oven over medium-high heat, stirring occasionally, 5 minutes or until thickened. Stir in broth and tomato juice. Add bay leaf and next 3 ingredients; bring to a boil. Reduce heat to medium-low, and simmer, partially covered and stirring occasionally, 20 minutes.

5. Add chicken; simmer, stirring occasionally, 5 to 7 minutes or until chicken is done.

6. Discard bay leaf. Stir in green onions and next 2 ingredients. Season with salt and pepper to taste. Divide queso fresco among 4 to 6 soup bowls. Ladle soup into bowls. Top with avocado and tortilla strips.

WESTERN OMELET QUESADILLAS

makes: 4 servings hands-on time: 30 min. total time: 30 min.

5   eggs

½   tsp. table salt

⅛   tsp. black pepper

½   cup diced cooked ham

¼   cup diced green bell pepper

¼   cup diced red bell pepper

2   to 3 Tbsp. butter, softened, divided

4   (6-in.) soft fajita-size flour tortillas

1¼   cups (5 oz.) shredded colby-Jack cheese blend

4   medium green onions, thinly sliced (¼ cup)

Salsa

1. Beat eggs, salt, and pepper in a medium bowl with wire whisk. Stir in ham and bell peppers. Melt 1 Tbsp. butter in a large skillet over medium-low heat. Add egg mixture. Cook 1 minute, gently lifting edges occasionally with spatula to allow uncooked egg mixture to flow to bottom of skillet. (Eggs will not be cooked at this point.) Continue to cook, lifting cooked portions until eggs are thickened but still moist. Remove egg mixture from skillet; keep warm. Wipe skillet clean.

2. Spread 1 to 2 Tbsp. remaining butter on 1 side of each tortilla. Place 1 tortilla in skillet, buttered side down. Top half of tortilla with one-fourth of egg mixture to within 1 inch of edge. Sprinkle one-fourth of cheese over egg mixture. Top with 1 Tbsp. of green onions; fold other half of tortilla over filling.

3. Increase heat to medium. Cook quesadilla 2 to 4 minutes, turning once, or until golden brown and cheese melts. Repeat with remaining tortillas, egg mixture, cheese, and onions. Serve warm with salsa.

BREAKFAST ON THE GO!

BRIE QUESADILLAS
WITH MANGO GUACAMOLE

makes: 24 servings hands-on time: 35 min. total time: 35 min.

Guacamole:

1	medium avocado, pitted, peeled, and quartered
½	small jalapeño pepper, seeded and finely chopped
1	small garlic clove, finely chopped
2	Tbsp. lime juice
¼	cup chopped fresh cilantro
⅛	tsp. table salt
½	medium mango, seed removed, peeled, and diced

Quesadillas:

1	(8-oz.) Brie round, cut into ⅛-inch strips (not wedges)
¼	lb. thinly sliced deli ham
6	(8-in.) soft taco-size flour tortillas
3	tsp. vegetable oil, divided

1. Place all guacamole ingredients except mango in a food processor. Cover; pulse 3 or 4 times until coarsely chopped. Spoon into small bowl; stir in mango. Press plastic wrap on guacamole to prevent it from turning brown. Refrigerate until serving time.

2. Place cheese and ham on half of each tortilla, fold other half of tortilla over and press down. Brush tops with 1 tsp. oil.

3. Heat a 12-inch skillet over medium-high heat. Place 3 quesadillas, oil sides down, in skillet. Brush tops with 1 tsp. oil. Cook 2 to 3 minutes, turning once, until golden brown and cheese melts. Repeat with remaining 3 quesadillas and 1 tsp. oil. Cut each quesadilla into 4 wedges. Serve with guacamole.

PESTO CHICKEN QUESADILLAS

makes: 4 servings   hands-on time: 12 min.   total time: 20 min.

1   **(3.5-oz.) jar pesto**

4   **(8-inch) soft taco-size flour tortillas**

1½ **cups shredded deli-roasted chicken**

1   **(8-oz.) package shredded Italian three-cheese blend**

Butter, softened

1. Spread about 1½ Tbsp. pesto on each tortilla. Sprinkle a slightly heaping ⅓ cup chicken onto half of each tortilla; sprinkle cheese over chicken on each tortilla. Fold each tortilla in half. Butter both sides of each folded tortilla.

2. Heat a large nonstick skillet over medium-high heat. Cook quesadillas, in 2 batches, 2 minutes on each side or until browned and crusty. Remove to a cutting board, and cut each quesadilla into 3 wedges.

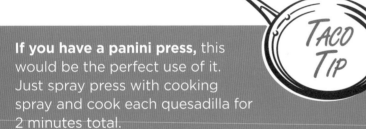

Taco Tip

If you have a panini press, this would be the perfect use of it. Just spray press with cooking spray and cook each quesadilla for 2 minutes total.

THIN & CRISPY!

OPEN-FACED CHILE-CHEESE QUESADILLAS

makes: 5 servings hands-on time: 10 min. total time: 30 min.

These quesadillas are open-faced, making them more like a thin-crust, Southwestern pizza!

5 (8-inch) soft taco-size flour tortillas

Olive oil

2 cups (8 oz.) shredded pepper Jack or Monterey Jack cheese

½ cup roasted red bell peppers (from 7-oz. jar), drained and finely chopped

½ cup pitted black olives, drained and chopped

1 to 2 chipotle peppers in adobo sauce (from 7-oz. can), chopped

1 tsp. adobo sauce (from can of chipotle peppers)

¼ cup finely chopped fresh cilantro

1. Preheat oven to 400°. Place tortillas on 2 large baking sheets. Brush tortillas lightly with oil; prick tortillas several times with a fork. Bake 6 minutes or until lightly browned and puffed. Cool.

2. Meanwhile, mix remaining ingredients. Sprinkle cheese mixture evenly over tortillas. Bake at 400° for 6 to 8 minutes or until cheese melts. Cut each tortilla into 6 wedges; serve warm.

Taco Tip

Turn these into traditional quesadillas by adding another tortilla on top. Gently press down and bake as directed.

HUEVOS RANCHEROS

makes: 4 servings   hands-on time: 29 min.   total time: 29 min.

1   cup chopped onion

1   cup chopped green, yellow, and red bell peppers

1   tsp. minced garlic

3   Tbsp. vegetable oil, divided

2   Tbsp. chopped fresh cilantro

½   tsp. table salt, divided

1   (14½-oz.) can diced zesty chili-style tomatoes, undrained

8   large eggs

½   cup refried beans, warmed

8   (6-inch) fajita-size corn or flour tortillas, warmed

¾   cup (6 oz.) shredded pepper Jack cheese

Hot sauce (optional)

Garnish: additional fresh cilantro

1. Sauté first 3 ingredients in 1 Tbsp. hot oil in a nonstick skillet over medium-high heat 5 minutes or until crisp-tender. Stir in 2 Tbsp. cilantro, ¼ tsp. salt, and tomatoes. Bring to a boil; reduce heat, and simmer, uncovered, 3 minutes or until thickened.

2. Meanwhile, heat 1 Tbsp. oil in a medium nonstick skillet over medium heat. Gently break 4 eggs into hot skillet; sprinkle with ⅛ tsp. salt. Cook, covered, 2 to 3 minutes or to desired degree of doneness. Transfer eggs to a plate. Repeat procedure with remaining 1 Tbsp. oil, remaining 4 eggs, and remaining ⅛ tsp. salt.

3. Spread refried beans over tortillas; top with tomato sauce. Top each serving with 1 egg, and sprinkle with cheese. Fold tortillas in half; serve immediately with hot sauce, if desired.

Omit homemade tomato sauce, and just use chunky salsa for an even speedier Huevos Rancheros.

SPEED IT UP!

BLACK BEAN ENCHILADAS

makes: 8 servings hands-on time: 15 min. total time: 45 min.

2 (15-oz.) cans black beans, drained and rinsed

1 tsp. chili powder

½ tsp. ground cumin

½ tsp. onion powder

½ tsp. garlic powder

1 (16-oz.) jar medium salsa

½ cup Monterey Jack queso dip

½ cup sour cream

8 (8-inch) soft taco-size flour tortillas

Toppings: shredded lettuce, chopped fresh cilantro, chopped tomato

1. Preheat oven to 350°. Mash 1 can of beans with a potato masher in a bowl; add remaining beans, chili powder, and next 3 ingredients, stirring until blended. Stir together salsa, queso dip, and sour cream in a bowl.

2. Spoon about ½ cup black bean mixture down center of each tortilla. Top each with 2 Tbsp. salsa mixture. Roll up tortillas, and place, seam sides down, in a lightly greased 13- x 9-inch baking dish. Pour remaining salsa mixture evenly over tortillas. Bake, covered, at 350° for 30 to 35 minutes or until thoroughly heated. Serve with desired toppings.

Skip mashing beans by substituting 1 can refried black beans. Stir in 1 can whole black beans and spices as directed in step 1.

SPEED IT UP!

CHICKEN ENCHILADAS

makes: 6 to 8 servings hands-on time: 25 min. total time: 2 hours, 45 min., including salsa

1   cup diced sweet onion

3   garlic cloves, minced

1   Tbsp. canola oil

2   cups chopped fresh baby spinach

2   (4.5-oz.) cans chopped green chiles, drained

3   cups shredded cooked chicken

1   (8-oz.) package ⅓-less-fat cream cheese, cubed and softened

2   cups (8 oz.) shredded pepper Jack cheese

⅓   cup chopped fresh cilantro

8   (8-inch) soft taco-size flour tortillas

Vegetable cooking spray

Tomatillo Salsa

TOMATILLO SALSA

makes: 3 cups
hands-on time: 10 min.
total time: 1 hour, 40 min.

2   cups diced tomatillo

⅓   cup sliced green onions

⅓   cup lightly packed fresh cilantro leaves

1   jalapeño pepper, seeded and finely chopped

1   Tbsp. fresh lime juice

½   tsp. table salt

1   cup diced avocado

1. Preheat oven to 350°. Sauté onion and garlic in hot oil in a large skillet over medium heat 5 minutes or until tender. Add spinach and green chiles; sauté 1 to 2 minutes or until spinach is wilted. Stir in chicken and next 3 ingredients, and cook, stirring constantly, 5 minutes or until cheeses melt. Add salt and pepper to taste. Spoon about ¾ cup chicken mixture down center of each tortilla; roll up tortillas.

2. Place rolled tortillas, seam sides down, in a lightly greased 13- x 9-inch baking dish. Lightly coat tortillas with cooking spray.

3. Bake at 350° for 30 to 35 minutes or until golden brown. Top with Tomatillo Salsa.

To make ahead: Prepare recipe as directed through Step 2. Cover and chill overnight. Let stand at room temperature 30 minutes. Uncover and proceed as directed in Step 3.

1. Stir together all ingredients except avocado. Cover and chill 1 to 4 hours. Let stand at room temperature 30 minutes. Stir in avocado just before serving.

SOUTHWESTERN CHIMICHANGAS

makes: 6 servings hands-on time: 20 min. total time: 20 min.

Who knew making chimichangas was this easy? Just load up your tortillas like a burrito, and fry for less than a minute.

½ **cup frozen chopped spinach, thawed**

1 **(11-oz.) can yellow corn with red and green bell peppers, drained**

1 **cup finely chopped deli-roasted chicken**

¼ **cup chopped green onions**

1 **Tbsp. taco seasoning mix**

6 **(8-inch) soft taco-size flour tortillas**

1 **cup (4 oz.) shredded pepper Jack cheese**

Peanut oil

Toppings: salsa, sour cream, chopped cilantro

1. Drain spinach well, pressing between paper towels.

2. Stir together spinach, corn, and next 3 ingredients in a medium-size, microwave-safe bowl. Microwave at HIGH 1 minute or until warm; stir well.

3. Warm tortillas in microwave according to package directions. Spoon about ½ cup chicken mixture just below center of each tortilla; sprinkle evenly with cheese. Fold opposite sides of tortilla over filling, and roll up. Secure with wooden picks. Flatten slightly with hand.

4. Pour peanut oil to a depth of 2 inches into a large heavy saucepan; heat to 375°. Fry chimichangas, in 3 batches, 30 seconds or just until golden brown; drain on paper towels. Serve with desired toppings. Remove wooden picks before serving.

COMPANY
WORTHY!

EASY TURKEY ENCHILADAS

makes: 4 servings hands-on time: 30 min. total time: 1 hour, 5 min.

Look for fresh salsa in the refrigerated section or the deli counter at your supermarket, or feel free to use your favorite jar of tomato salsa.

1   lb. ground turkey sausage*

½   cup chopped onion

1   tsp. minced garlic

1   (7.76-oz.) can tomatillo salsa, divided

¼   cup chopped fresh cilantro

8   (6-inch) fajita-size corn tortillas**

2   cups (8 oz.) shredded Mexican four-cheese blend, divided

Vegetable cooking spray

2   cups refrigerated fresh medium-heat tomato salsa

½   cup low-sodium chicken broth

Garnish: chopped fresh cilantro

1. Preheat oven to 350°. Brown sausage in a large skillet over medium-high heat, stirring occasionally, 11 to 14 minutes or until meat crumbles and is no longer pink. Remove sausage from skillet using a slotted spoon, and drain on paper towels.

2. Sauté onion and garlic in hot drippings over medium-high heat 2 to 3 minutes or until onion is tender. Remove from heat. Stir in sausage, ½ cup tomatillo salsa, and ¼ cup chopped cilantro.

3. Place 2 tortillas between damp paper towels. Microwave tortillas at HIGH 15 seconds. Repeat procedure with remaining tortillas.

4. Spoon about ⅓ cup sausage mixture evenly down center of each softened tortilla, and sprinkle each with 1 Tbsp. cheese; roll tortillas up, and place, seam sides down, in a lightly greased 13- x 9-inch baking dish. Lightly coat tops of tortillas with cooking spray.

5. Bake at 350° for 20 to 25 minutes or until tortillas are crisp.

6. Stir together tomato salsa, chicken broth, and remaining tomatillo salsa in a medium saucepan over medium-high heat; cook, stirring occasionally, 4 to 6 minutes or until thoroughly heated. Pour salsa mixture over tortillas, and top evenly with remaining cheese. Bake 5 more minutes or until cheese melts. Let stand 5 minutes.

* Ground pork sausage may be substituted.

** 8 (6-inch) fajita-size flour tortillas may be substituted, omitting Step 3.

Note: We tested with La Costeña Green Mexican Salsa for tomatillo salsa.

LAYERED MEXICAN TORTILLA PIE

makes: 6 to 8 servings   hands-on time: 15 min.   total time: 3 hours, 30 min.

1   **Tbsp. canola oil**

½   **cup refrigerated prechopped onion**

1   **(12-oz.) package frozen meatless burger crumbles**

½   **tsp. chili powder**

½   **tsp. ground cumin**

2   **(11-oz.) cans yellow corn with red and green bell peppers, drained**

Heavy-duty aluminum foil

1   **(16-oz.) can refried beans**

6   **(6-inch) flour tortillas**

1⅔   **cups fresh salsa**

2¾   **cups shredded Monterey Jack cheese**

Toppings: sour cream, chopped fresh cilantro, shredded Monterey Jack cheese, fresh salsa, guacamole

1. Heat oil in a large nonstick skillet over medium-high heat. Add onion; cook 3 minutes or until tender. Stir in burger crumbles and next 3 ingredients. Cook 2 minutes or until crumbles thaw. Remove from heat.

2. Fold 2 (17- x 12-inch) sheets of heavy-duty aluminum foil into 2 (17- x 2-inch) strips. Arrange strips in an X pattern in a lightly greased 4-qt. round slow cooker, allowing foil to extend 1 inch beyond edges of slow cooker.

3. Spread about ⅓ cup refried beans on 1 side of each of 5 tortillas. Place 1 tortilla, bean side up, atop foil X in slow cooker. Spoon 1 cup burger mixture over beans; top with ⅓ cup salsa and ½ cup cheese. Repeat layers 4 times. Top with remaining tortilla, and sprinkle with remaining ¼ cup cheese. Cover and cook on LOW 3 hours or until cheese melts and edges are bubbly.

4. Remove insert from slow cooker; let stand, uncovered, 15 minutes. Grasping ends of foil strips, carefully transfer pie to a serving plate. Carefully remove foil strips. Cut pie into wedges, and serve with desired toppings.

Note: We tested with MorningStar Farms® Meal Starters Grillers® Recipe Crumbles™.

VEGETARIAN!

SKILLET-GRILLED BURRITOS

makes: 8 servings hands-on time: 28 min. total time: 40 min., including sauce

2 cups chopped cooked chicken breast

1 (15-oz.) can black beans, drained and rinsed

1 (11-oz.) can yellow corn with red and green bell peppers, drained

1 cup (4 oz.) shredded 2% reduced-fat Cheddar cheese

Creamy Cilantro-Jalapeño Sauce, divided

8 (8-inch) soft taco-size whole wheat flour tortillas, warmed

Vegetable cooking spray

Salsa

1. Toss together first 4 ingredients and ½ cup Creamy Cilantro-Jalapeño Sauce. Spread ¾ cup chicken mixture just below center of each tortilla. Fold opposite sides of tortillas over filling, and roll up. Coat burritos with cooking spray.

2. Coat a hot griddle or nonstick skillet with cooking spray. Cook burritos, in batches, on hot griddle over medium heat, pressing gently with a spatula, 3 to 4 minutes on each side or until golden brown and cheese melts. Serve with salsa and remaining Creamy Cilantro-Jalapeño Sauce.

CREAMY CILANTRO-JALAPEÑO SAUCE

makes: 1¼ cups
hands-on time: 10 min.
total time: 40 min.

1 cup light sour cream

½ cup loosely packed fresh cilantro leaves, chopped

2 Tbsp. diced pickled jalapeño peppers

2 tsp. chopped yellow onion

2 tsp. Dijon mustard

1 tsp. lime zest

1. Stir together all ingredients in a small bowl. Cover and chill 30 minutes. Store in an airtight container up to 2 days.

AUTHENTIC ENCHILADA PIES

makes: 4 servings   hands-on time: 30 min.   total time: 50 min.

1   (2-oz.) package dried hibiscus flowers, picked through

1   cup thinly sliced sweet onion

1½ cups chopped bell pepper

1½ cups chopped zucchini

¼   cup olive oil

1   (15-oz.) can black beans, drained, rinsed, and mashed

1   Tbsp. sugar

1   tsp. kosher salt

1   tsp. dried oregano

¼   tsp. dried thyme

1   cup vegetable broth

12 (6-inch) fajita-size corn tortillas*

1¼ cups (5 oz.) shredded Monterey Jack cheese

5   cups jarred enchilada sauce

½   cup (2 oz.) crumbled queso fresco (fresh Mexican cheese)

Toppings: sour cream, chopped red onion, fresh cilantro leaves

1. Preheat oven to 350°. Bring flowers and 2 cups water to a simmer in a small saucepan over medium heat. Remove from heat; cover and let stand 5 to 8 minutes or until flowers are plump. Drain flowers, and coarsely chop.

2. Sauté flowers, onion, and next 2 ingredients in hot oil in a large skillet over medium heat 10 minutes or until vegetables are tender. Stir in beans and next 4 ingredients, and cook, stirring often, 2 minutes.

3. Pour broth into a shallow dish. Dip 4 tortillas, 1 at a time, in broth, and place 1 inch apart on a foil-lined 15- x 10-inch jelly-roll pan. Divide half of hibiscus mixture among tortillas; top each with about 2 Tbsp. Monterey Jack cheese and ¼ cup warm enchilada sauce. Repeat layers once; top each stack with a tortilla. Spoon ¼ cup enchilada sauce over each stack.

4. Bake at 350° for 20 minutes or until bubbly.

5. Microwave remaining enchilada sauce in a microwave-safe bowl at HIGH 1 minute or until warm. Spoon over stacks. Sprinkle with queso fresco and remaining Monterey Jack cheese. Serve with enchilada sauce and toppings.

* 20 (4-inch) corn tortillas may be substituted. Add 2 more layers, and divide filling accordingly.

Note: Find dried hibiscus flowers (Flor de Jamaica) at Hispanic markets and amazon.com. You may omit them, if desired.

TORTILLA CASSEROLE

makes: 8 servings hands-on time: 10 min. total time: 4 hours, 10 min.

2 (10-oz.) cans mild green chile enchilada sauce, divided

10 (6-inch) corn tortillas, torn into 3-inch pieces

4 cups shredded cooked chicken breasts

1½ cups sour cream

3 cups shredded colby-Jack cheese blend, divided

1 (10¾-oz.) can cream of mushroom soup

8 cups shredded iceberg lettuce

1 (15-oz.) can black beans, drained and rinsed

3 tomatoes, diced

1. Spoon ½ cup enchilada sauce over bottom of a greased 4-qt. slow cooker. Add enough tortilla pieces to cover sauce.

2. Stir together chicken, sour cream, 2 cups cheese, and soup. Spread 2 cups chicken mixture over tortilla pieces. Top with tortilla pieces to cover. Drizzle with ½ cup enchilada sauce. Repeat layers twice, ending with tortilla pieces and remaining enchilada sauce. Sprinkle with remaining 1 cup cheese.

3. Cover and cook on LOW 4 hours. Place lettuce on plates; top with chicken mixture, beans, and tomatoes. Serve hot.

LITTLE HELPERS

This recipe is super easy, and it's a great one for the kids to master. Just have an adult nearby for cooking in the slow cooker.

SOUTHWEST CORNBREAD CASSEROLE

makes: 8 servings hands-on time: 20 min. total time: 55 min.

These individual casseroles are the Southwest version of a pot pie. Cornbread muffin mix is the secret for getting these made in a hurry.

2   tsp. vegetable oil

3   medium onions, chopped (1½ cups)

1   (15-oz.) can black beans, drained and rinsed

1   (11-oz.) can whole kernel corn with red and green peppers, drained

1   (10-oz.) can diced tomatoes and green chiles, drained

1   (10-oz.) can enchilada sauce

½   cup salsa

2   cups chopped cooked chicken

¼   cup chopped fresh cilantro

2   (6.5-oz.) packages cornbread & muffin mix

⅓   cup milk

4   large eggs

1½   cups (6 oz.) shredded Mexican four-cheese blend

Garnish: fresh jalapeño peppers, sliced

1. Preheat oven to 350°. Spray 8 (8-oz.) individual baking dishes with cooking spray. Heat oil in a large skillet over medium heat. Cook onions in oil 5 minutes, stirring occasionally, until tender.

2. Mix beans and next 4 ingredients in a large bowl. Stir in chicken, cilantro, and onions. Spoon mixture into baking dishes.

3. Stir muffin mix, milk, and eggs in a medium bowl just until moistened. Spoon topping by heaping spoonfuls over chicken mixture.

4. Bake, uncovered, at 350° for 20 to 25 minutes or until filling is bubbly and topping is golden brown. Sprinkle with cheese blend. Bake 5 more minutes or until cheese melts.

SLOW-COOKER ENCHILADA CASSEROLE

makes: 6 servings hands-on time: 14 min. total time: 4 hours, 19 min.

3   Tbsp. diced green chiles, divided

½   cup mild salsa

¼   cup chopped green onions

¼   cup chopped fresh cilantro

1   (15-oz.) can black beans, drained

1   (11-oz.) can yellow corn with red and green bell peppers, drained

1   (10-oz.) can enchilada sauce

2   large eggs

2   Tbsp. chopped jarred roasted red bell peppers

1   (8½-oz.) package corn muffin mix

1½ cups (6 oz.) shredded Mexican four-cheese blend

Garnishes: sour cream, chopped fresh cilantro

1. Stir together 2 Tbsp. green chiles and next 6 ingredients in a lightly greased 4-qt. slow cooker. Cover and cook on LOW 3 hours.

2. Whisk eggs in a medium bowl; stir in remaining 1 Tbsp. green chiles, roasted bell peppers, and muffin mix. Spoon batter over bean mixture in slow cooker. Cover and cook on LOW 1 hour or until cornbread is done.

3. Sprinkle cheese over cornbread. Increase heat to HIGH; cover and cook 5 minutes or until cheese melts. Spoon into shallow bowls.

Taco Tip

This recipe is relatively mild as is but could be spiced up with hot salsa and hot enchilada sauce. Try substituting chopped pickled jalapeño peppers for the roasted red bell peppers for a jalapeño cornbread topping.

COATED IN CRUNCH!

TORTILLA-CRUSTED PORK

makes: 6 servings hands-on time: 32 min. total time: 1 hour 47 min., including Pico de Gallo

2 **lb. pork tenderloin**

½ **cup finely crushed blue-corn tortilla chips**

½ **cup finely crushed tortilla chips**

1 **Tbsp. coarsely ground black pepper**

½ **tsp. chili powder**

½ **tsp. table salt**

¼ **tsp. ground cumin**

3 **Tbsp. extra virgin olive oil, divided**

Pico de Gallo

Garnish: fresh cilantro sprigs; jalapeño peppers, sliced

1. Remove silver skin from tenderloin, leaving a thin layer of fat. Cut tenderloin into 1-inch-thick medallions.

2. Combine blue-corn tortilla chips and next 5 ingredients in a bowl. Brush pork medallions with 1½ Tbsp. olive oil, and dredge in tortilla chip mixture, pressing mixture into medallions on all sides to thoroughly coat.

3. Cook pork medallions in remaining 1½ Tbsp. hot oil in a large skillet over medium heat 6 minutes on each side or until done. Serve with Pico de Gallo.

PICO DE GALLO

makes: 3 cups
hands-on time: 10 min.
total time: 1 hour, 10 min.

2 **medium tomatoes, seeded and diced**

1 **medium avocado, diced**

¼ **cup diced white onion**

1 **serrano or jalapeño pepper, seeded and finely chopped**

2 **Tbsp. lime juice**

1 **Tbsp. extra virgin olive oil**

1. Toss together all ingredients in a medium bowl. Cover and chill 1 hour. Season with salt to taste.

Let the pork sear evenly on each side to allow the coating to reach maximum crispness.

Taco Tip

GRILLED STEAK
WITH PINEAPPLE SALSA

makes: 4 servings hands-on time: 15 min. total time: 15 min.

Vegetable cooking spray

1 **(8-oz.) can pineapple slices in juice, drained**

2 **Tbsp. brown sugar**

½ **tsp. kosher salt, divided**

1 **(1-lb.) flat-iron steak**

2 **green onions**

½ **cup chunky salsa**

Precooked rice

Garnish: grilled green onion

1. Coat cold cooking grate of grill with cooking spray, and place on grill. Preheat grill to 350° to 400° (medium-high) heat.

2. Sprinkle pineapple with brown sugar and ¼ tsp. salt. Sprinkle steak with remaining ¼ tsp. salt. Grill steak, pineapple, and green onions, covered, 3 to 4 minutes on each side or until steak is desired degree of doneness and pineapple and green onions are tender.

3. Let steak stand 5 minutes; cut diagonally across grain into thin slices. Finely chop pineapple and green onions; place in a small bowl, and stir in salsa. Serve steak over rice and top with pineapple salsa. Garnish with grilled green onion, if desired.

Grilling the pineapple slices and green onions alongside the meat preps them simultaneously for a quick stir into bottled salsa to serve over steaks.

SPEED IT UP!

MIXED GRILL
WITH CILANTRO PESTO

makes: 8 servings   hands-on time: 10 min.   total time: 35 min., including pesto

---

4   (1½-inch-thick) center-cut bone-in pork chops

4   (6-oz.) beef tenderloin fillets (about 2 inches thick)

Cilantro Pesto

Garnishes: fresh cilantro sprigs, rosemary sprigs, chives

1. Sprinkle pork chops and beef fillets evenly with desired amount of salt and pepper.

2. Grill chops and fillets, covered with grill lid, over medium-high heat (350° to 400°). Grill chops 8 to 10 minutes on each side or until done. Grill fillets 8 to 10 minutes. Turn fillets over, and cook 5 more minutes or to desired degree of doneness. Remove chops and fillets from grill, and let stand 5 minutes. Serve with Cilantro Pesto.

CILANTRO PESTO

makes: about ¾ cup
hands-on time: 10 min.
total time: 10 min.

½   cup loosely packed fresh cilantro leaves

½   cup loosely packed fresh flat-leaf parsley

2   garlic cloves

¼   cup (1 oz.) freshly grated Parmesan cheese

2   Tbsp. toasted pumpkin seeds

¼   tsp. table salt

¼   cup olive oil

1. Pulse first 6 ingredients in a food processor 10 times or just until chopped. Drizzle olive oil over mixture, and pulse 6 more times or until a coarse mixture forms. Cover and chill until ready to serve.

Kid's Fiesta

Have fun with dinner
by making one of these
family-favorite dishes.

TACOS TO GO!

SPICY SOUTHWESTERN MUFFINS

makes: 8 servings hands-on time: 15 min. total time: 40 min.

¼ lb. spicy pork sausage, casings removed

1 (8-oz.) can refrigerated crescent rolls or dinner rolls

1 Tbsp. chopped fresh cilantro

1 egg

1 Tbsp. milk

½ tsp. taco seasoning mix

½ cup (2 oz.) shredded pepper Jack cheese

Garnishes: salsa, sour cream, additional chopped fresh cilantro

1. Preheat oven to 375°. Lightly grease 8 cups of 12-cup muffin pan.

2. Cook sausage in an 8-inch skillet over medium-high heat for 5 minutes, stirring occasionally, until meat crumbles and is no longer pink; drain.

3. Remove crescent rolls from package (if using), but do not unroll. Using serrated knife, cut roll into 8 rounds; carefully separate rounds. Press 1 round on bottom and completely up side of each muffin cup. If using refrigerated dinner rolls, separate into 8 rounds, and press into muffin cups.

4. Mix sausage and 1 Tbsp. cilantro in a small bowl. Beat egg, milk, and taco seasoning with a fork in a separate small bowl until blended. Spoon about 1 Tbsp. sausage mixture into each dough-lined muffin cup. Divide egg mixture evenly among cups. Sprinkle with cheese.

5. Bake at 375° for 14 to 16 minutes or until filling is set and edges are golden brown. Cool 5 minutes. Run knife around edge of cups to loosen; remove muffins from pan. Serve warm.

Taco Tip

These also make for the perfect snack or breakfast on the go! Just package in aluminum foil to keep them warm.

SLOW-COOKER BEEF NACHOS

makes: 6 servings hands-on time: 38 min. total time: 8 hours, 48 min.

1 (3-lb.) boneless beef rump roast

1 Tbsp. vegetable oil

1 (12-oz.) jar mild banana pepper rings, drained

1 (16-oz.) can beef broth

3 garlic cloves, minced

Tortilla chips

1 (15-oz.) can black beans, drained and rinsed

Toppings: chopped tomatoes, finely chopped onions, shredded Monterey Jack cheese

Garnishes: cilantro, avocado, sour cream

1. Season roast with desired amount of salt and pepper. Brown all sides of roast in hot oil in a large skillet over high heat. Place in a 6-qt. slow cooker. Add banana pepper rings, beef broth, and garlic. Cover and cook on LOW 8 hours or until fork-tender.

2. Transfer roast to a cutting board, reserving liquid in slow cooker. Shred roast using two forks; return to slow cooker. Keep warm on LOW.

3. Preheat oven to 350°. Place tortilla chips on a baking sheet; top with shredded beef, black beans, tomatoes, onions, and cheese. Bake 10 minutes.

SOUTHWEST CORNDOG BITES

makes: 36 bites hands-on time: 10 min. total time: 30 min.

Vegetable cooking spray

1   (6.5-oz.) package yellow cornbread & muffin mix

⅓   cup milk

2   Tbsp. butter or margarine, melted

1   large egg

1   (4.5-oz.) can chopped green chiles, drained

1   cup (4 oz.) shredded Monterey Jack cheese

¼   cup chopped green onions (4 medium)

15 cocktail-size smoked link turkey sausages (from 14-oz. package), sliced (1 cup)

Ketchup and mustard

1. Preheat oven to 375°. Place mini paper baking cups in 36 cups of 2 (24-cup) mini muffin pans. Coat cups with cooking spray.

2. Stir muffin mix and next 6 ingredients in a medium bowl just until moistened (batter will be lumpy). Stir in sausages. Divide batter evenly among muffin cups.

3. Bake at 375° for 15 minutes or until golden brown. Cool 5 minutes; remove from pans to cooling racks. Serve warm with ketchup and mustard.

To add a little more heat to these corn dog bites, use pepper Jack cheese in place of Monterey Jack.

TACO Tip

PARTY PERFECT!

PEPPER AND CHICKEN "NACHOS"

makes: 4 servings   hands-on time: 12 min.   total time: 37 min.

4   garlic cloves, pressed
¼   cup cider vinegar
⅓   cup olive oil
½   tsp. ground cumin
½   tsp. table salt
½   tsp. freshly ground black pepper
4   medium-size red bell peppers, cut into 2-inch pieces

2   cups chopped deli-roasted chicken
1   (15½-oz.) can black-eyed peas, drained and rinsed
1   (8-oz.) pkg. shredded sharp Cheddar cheese
⅓   cup loosely packed fresh cilantro leaves

1. Preheat grill to 350° to 400° (medium-high) heat. Combine garlic and next 5 ingredients. Reserve 3 Tbsp. garlic mixture. Pour remaining garlic mixture into a large shallow dish; add peppers, turning to coat. Cover and chill 15 minutes, turning once. Remove peppers from marinade, reserving marinade for basting.

2. Grill peppers, covered with grill lid, 4 to 5 minutes or until grill marks appear and peppers are slightly tender, turning occasionally and basting with marinade.

3. Preheat broiler with oven rack 4 inches from heat. Combine chicken and peas with reserved 3 Tbsp. garlic mixture. Place peppers in a single layer on a lightly greased rack in an aluminum foil–lined broiler pan. Top each pepper with chicken mixture. Sprinkle peppers evenly with cheese.

4. Broil 4 to 5 minutes or until cheese is melted. Remove from oven, sprinkle with cilantro, and serve immediately.

EASY QUESADILLAS

makes: 8 servings hands-on time: 5 min. total time: 8 min.

Quesadillas don't get any easier than this. Top two flour tortillas with canned refried beans, shredded Mexican cheese, taco sauce, and two more flour tortillas. Microwave and cut into wedges for a snack or light supper.

¾ **cup refried beans with sausage**

4 **(8-inch) flour tortillas**

1¼ **cups (5 oz.) shredded Mexican four-cheese blend, divided**

½ **cup taco sauce, divided**

Sour cream

1. Spread beans evenly over 2 tortillas. Sprinkle evenly with ¾ cup cheese, and drizzle with ¼ cup taco sauce. Top with remaining tortillas.

2. Microwave 1 quesadilla, covered with a paper towel, on a microwave-safe plate at HIGH 1 to 1½ minutes. Repeat procedure with remaining quesadilla.

3. Cut each into 8 wedges; serve with remaining ¼ cup taco sauce, sour cream, and remaining ½ cup cheese.

Taco Tip

For a crispy quesadilla, place microwaved quesadillas in a lightly greased skillet over medium heat and cook on both sides until toasted.

SUPER EASY!

BARBECUED PORK QUESADILLAS

makes: 4 servings hands-on time: 26 min. total time: 26 min.

1 lb. chopped barbecued pork (without sauce)

1 cup barbecue sauce

½ cup chopped fresh cilantro

2 green onions, minced

8 (6-inch) fajita-size flour tortillas

1 (8-oz.) package shredded Mexican four-cheese blend

Toppings: sour cream, sliced green onions, barbecue sauce

1. Stir together barbecued pork and next 3 ingredients.

2. Place 1 tortilla in a hot lightly greased skillet or griddle. Sprinkle tortilla with ¼ cup cheese, and spoon ⅓ cup pork mixture on half of tortilla. Cook 2 to 3 minutes or until cheese melts. Fold tortilla in half over filling; transfer to a serving plate. Repeat procedure with remaining tortillas, cheese, and pork mixture. Serve with desired toppings.

Taco Tip

For an easy side, melt a few tablespoons of butter with minced garlic and a dash of chili powder in a microwave-safe bowl; pour over boiled or grilled corn on the cob.

EASY SKILLET TACOS

makes: 4 to 6 servings hands-on time: 25 min. total time: 40 min.

Tacos are an easy go-to on a busy weeknight; all you have to do is prepare the beef and chop the toppings, and everyone can make their own tacos.

1   lb. ground beef

1   small onion, chopped

1   tsp. olive oil

1   Tbsp. chili powder

1½   tsp. ground cumin

1   tsp. table salt

1   (15-oz.) can pinto beans, drained and rinsed

1   (8-oz.) can tomato sauce

½   cup salsa

1½   cups (6 oz.) shredded Cheddar cheese

1   Tbsp. chopped fresh cilantro

Taco shells or flour tortillas, warmed

Toppings: shredded lettuce, diced tomatoes, salsa, sour cream

1. Cook ground beef in a large skillet over medium-high heat, stirring until beef crumbles and is no longer pink. Drain well. Remove beef; wipe skillet with a paper towel.

2. Sauté onion in hot oil in same skillet over medium-high heat. Add chili powder, cumin, salt, and beef. Cook 5 to 7 minutes, stirring occasionally. Stir in beans, tomato sauce, ¾ cup water, and salsa. Mash pinto beans in skillet with a fork, leaving some beans whole. Bring to a boil; reduce heat, and simmer, uncovered, 8 to 10 minutes or until liquid is reduced.

3. Top with cheese and cilantro. Cover, turn off heat, and let stand 5 minutes or until cheese melts. Serve with taco shells or tortillas and desired toppings.

TEMPURA SHRIMP TACOS

makes: 6 servings hands-on time: 35 min. total time: 1 hour, 15 min., including coleslaw

---

1 **lb. unpeeled, large raw shrimp**

1 **cup tempura batter mix**

¾ **cup cold light beer**

2 **tsp. fajita seasoning**

Vegetable oil

12 **(6-inch) fajita-size flour tortillas, warmed**

Mexi-Coleslaw Mix

Toppings: chopped tomatoes, sliced avocados, chopped fresh cilantro

1. Peel shrimp; devein, if desired.

2. Whisk together tempura batter mix, beer, and fajita seasoning in a large bowl; let stand 5 minutes.

3. Pour oil to depth of 2 inches into a Dutch oven; heat to 325°. Dip shrimp in tempura batter, shaking off excess. Fry shrimp, in batches, 1 to 2 minutes on each side or until golden; drain on a wire rack over paper towels.

4. Serve in warm tortillas with Mexi-Coleslaw Mix and desired toppings.

Note: We tested with McCormick Golden Dipt Tempura Seafood Batter Mix.

MEXI-COLESLAW MIX

makes: 6 servings
hands-on time: 10 min.
total time: 40 min.

---

2 **Tbsp. chopped fresh cilantro**

3 **Tbsp. mayonnaise**

1 **Tbsp. fresh lime juice**

½ **tsp. fajita seasoning**

½ **(16-oz.) package shredded coleslaw mix**

1. Stir together first 4 ingredients in a large bowl; add shredded coleslaw mix, stirring to coat. Season with salt to taste. Cover and chill 30 minutes to 24 hours.

Make the coleslaw up to 24 hours in advance to jump-start this recipe.

Speed It Up!

CRISPY ROLLUPS!

TAQUITOS
WITH PORK PICADILLO

makes: 6 to 8 servings hands-on time: 15 min. total time: 33 min.

Flour tortillas are best in this recipe (rather than corn) because they are easier to fill, roll, and secure; plus they tend to fry up a bit more airy and crisp than their corn cousins.

- 12 (6-inch) flour tortillas
- 1 lb. chopped cooked pork*
- 2 Tbsp. vegetable oil, divided
- 1 medium onion, chopped
- 4 garlic cloves, minced
- 3 jalapeño peppers, seeded and chopped
- ¼ cup tomato paste
- ¼ cup red wine vinegar
- 1 tsp. black pepper
- ½ tsp. table salt
- ¼ cup chopped fresh cilantro
- 1 cup (4 oz.) shredded Monterey Jack cheese

Vegetable oil

Toppings: shredded lettuce, salsa, cilantro, finely chopped red onion

1. Heat tortillas according to package directions. Cut tortillas into circles with a 3-inch cutter. Put tortilla circles on a plate, and cover with a towel; set aside.

2. Cook pork in a large nonstick skillet in 1 Tbsp. hot vegetable oil over medium heat 5 minutes or until lightly browned, stirring constantly. Remove pork from pan, and drain on paper towels. Wipe skillet clean.

3. Sauté onion, garlic, and peppers in remaining 1 Tbsp. hot oil over medium-high heat 3 to 4 minutes or until onion is tender. Stir in pork, tomato paste, vinegar, pepper, and salt; cook, stirring occasionally, 2 to 3 minutes. Remove from heat, and stir in chopped cilantro.

4. Spoon 2 Tbsp. pork mixture down center of each tortilla circle; top evenly with cheese. Roll up, and secure with a wooden pick.

5. Pour vegetable oil to depth of 1½ inches into a large heavy skillet. Fry taquitos, in batches, in hot oil (350°) over medium-high heat 1 to 2 minutes or until golden brown. Remove wooden picks, and serve immediately. Serve with desired toppings.

* 1 lb. chopped or shredded pork (without sauce) from your favorite barbecue restaurant may be used.

SIZZLING GRILLED CHICKEN TOSTADAS

makes: 8 servings   hands-on time: 50 min.   total time: 1 hour, 55 min.

3   Tbsp. olive oil

2   Tbsp. lime juice

4   tsp. Montreal chicken grill seasoning

4   tsp. Asian hot chili sauce (such as Sriracha), divided

4   boneless skinless chicken breasts (about 1¼ lb.)

Vegetable cooking spray

1   (15-oz.) can refried black beans

8   tostada shells (from 4.5-oz. box)

1   (14-oz.) package refrigerated guacamole

2   cups (8 oz.) shredded Mexican four-cheese blend

½   cup taco sauce

4   cups shredded iceberg lettuce

1. Mix oil, lime juice, grill seasoning, and 3 tsp. Asian hot chili sauce in a 1-gal. heavy-duty zip-top plastic bag. Add chicken; seal bag and turn to coat. Refrigerate 1 hour to marinate.

2. Coat cold cooking grate of grill with cooking spray, and place on grill. Preheat grill to 300° to 400° (medium-high) heat. Remove chicken from marinade; discard marinade. Place chicken on cooking grate and cover. Cook 12 to 14 minutes, turning once, until juice of chicken is clear when pierced with a fork (at least 165°). Cool slightly; chop chicken.

3. To assemble tostadas, spread refried beans over tostada shells. Spread guacamole over beans. Top evenly with chicken and cheese. Stir remaining 1 tsp. Asian hot chili sauce into taco sauce; drizzle over tostadas. Place tostadas on grill and cover. Cook 2 to 3 minutes or until cheese is melted. Top with lettuce. Serve immediately.

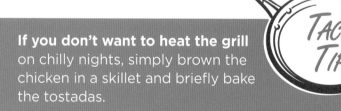

If you don't want to heat the grill on chilly nights, simply brown the chicken in a skillet and briefly bake the tostadas.

Taco Tip

BEEF AND CHICKEN FAJITAS

makes: 10 servings hands-on time: 15 min. total time: 6 hours, 15 min.

1½ **lb. flat-iron steak, cut into strips**

1 **lb. skinned and boned chicken breasts, cut into strips**

1 **tsp. table salt**

1 **tsp. black pepper**

1½ **Tbsp. fajita seasoning, divided**

¼ **cup olive oil, divided**

3 **Tbsp. fresh lime juice**

2 **Tbsp. Worcestershire sauce**

5 **large garlic cloves, minced**

1½ **(1-lb.) packages frozen pepper stir-fry**

10 **(8-inch) flour tortillas, warmed**

Lime wedges (optional)

Toppings: guacamole, shredded lettuce, chopped tomato, shredded Cheddar cheese

1. Place steak and chicken strips on separate plates; sprinkle with salt, pepper, and 1 Tbsp. fajita seasoning.

2. Heat 1 Tbsp. oil in an extra-large skillet over medium-high heat. Add steak to pan; cook 3 minutes or until browned, turning once. Place steak in a 5- or 6-qt. slow cooker. Add chicken to pan; cook over medium-high heat 3 minutes or until browned, stirring once. Add chicken to steak in slow cooker.

3. Stir together remaining 3 Tbsp. oil, lime juice, Worcestershire sauce, garlic, and remaining 1½ tsp. fajita seasoning in a small bowl; pour over chicken and steak in slow cooker. Cover and cook on LOW 5 hours or until meat is tender. Stir in frozen pepper stir-fry. Cover and cook 1 to 2 more hours.

4. Spoon filling into tortillas and, if desired, squeeze lime wedges over filling. Serve with desired toppings.

BAKED CHICKEN CHIMICHANGAS

makes: 20 chimichangas hands-on time: 40 min. total time: 53 min.

Make these Tex-Mex chimichangas for a dinner your whole family will love. Top with your favorite picante sauce, salsa, or guacamole.

1 (16-oz.) jar picante sauce or salsa, divided

7 cups chopped cooked chicken

1 small onion, diced

2 to 2½ tsp. ground cumin

1½ tsp. dried oregano

1 tsp. table salt

20 (8-inch) flour tortillas

3 cups (12 oz.) shredded Cheddar cheese

Vegetable cooking spray

Toppings: guacamole, sour cream, shredded lettuce, diced tomatoes

1. Preheat oven to 425°.

2. Combine 1½ cups picante sauce and next 5 ingredients in a Dutch oven; cook over medium-low heat, stirring often, 25 minutes or until most of liquid evaporates. Spoon ⅓ cup mixture below center of each tortilla; top each with 2 Tbsp. cheese.

3. Fold in 2 sides of tortillas to enclose filling. Fold over top and bottom edges of tortillas, making rectangles. Secure with wooden picks. Place, folded side down, on greased baking sheets. Coat chimichangas with cooking spray.

4. Bake at 425° for 8 minutes; turn and bake 5 more minutes. Remove picks; top with remaining picante sauce and desired toppings.

BAKED, NOT FRIED!

CHICKEN AND BLACK BEAN ENCHILADAS

makes: 4 to 6 servings hands-on time: 10 min. total time: 45 min.

3 cups shredded deli-roasted chicken

1 (15-oz.) can black beans, drained and rinsed

1 (10-oz.) can diced tomatoes and green chiles, undrained

1 (8¾-oz.) can no-salt-added corn, drained

1 (8-oz.) package shredded reduced-fat Mexican four-cheese blend (2 cups), divided

8 (8-inch) whole wheat flour tortillas

Cooking spray

2 (10-oz.) cans enchilada sauce

1. Preheat oven to 350°.

2. Combine first 4 ingredients and 1½ cups cheese in a large bowl. Spoon chicken mixture evenly down the center of each tortilla, and roll up. Arrange, seam side down, in a 13- x 9-inch baking dish coated with cooking spray.

3. Pour enchilada sauce evenly over tortillas, and sprinkle evenly with remaining ½ cup cheese.

4. Bake, covered, at 350° for 20 minutes. Remove foil, and bake 15 more minutes or until bubbly.

Make this a meal by serving heat-and-serve Spanish rice alongside. Stir in some chopped cilantro for extra flavor.

Taco Tip

NACHO POT PIE

makes: 8 servings   hands-on time: 25 min.   total time: 50 min.

3 cups chicken broth

½ cup butter or margarine

2 medium carrots, cut into ¼-inch slices

2 shallots, finely chopped (½ cup)

3 garlic cloves, finely chopped

2 Tbsp. taco seasoning mix

¾ tsp. freshly ground black pepper

½ tsp. table salt

½ cup all-purpose flour

¼ cup whipping cream

2 cups shredded deli-roasted chicken

1 (15-oz.) can black beans, drained and rinsed

1 (12-oz.) bag frozen corn, thawed

4 cups crushed tortilla chips

1 cup (4 oz.) shredded Mexican cheese blend

1. Preheat oven to 375°.

2. Heat broth in a 4-qt. saucepan over medium-high heat. Remove from heat; cover to keep warm.

3. Melt butter with 2 Tbsp. of warm broth in a Dutch oven over medium-high heat. Add carrots and next 5 ingredients. Cook 5 minutes, stirring occasionally, until carrots are tender. Gradually add flour, stirring with whisk. Cook 1 to 2 minutes, stirring constantly. Stir in whipping cream and remaining warm broth. Heat to boiling; add chicken, beans, and corn. Reduce heat; simmer, uncovered, for 5 minutes, stirring occasionally, until slightly thickened.

4. Spoon mixture into ungreased 11- x 7-inch (2-qt.) baking dish. Top with crushed tortilla chips. Sprinkle with cheese. Bake, uncovered, at 375° for 20 to 25 minutes or until golden brown.

Let the kids crush the tortilla chips and sprinkle them over to make a creative crunchy topping that everyone will love.

LITTLE HELPERS

MEXICAN PIZZA

makes: 6 servings hands-on time: 20 min. total time: 40 min.

Sliced chorizo, fresh cilantro, and corn give this pizza a zesty makeover!

1   (13.8-oz.) can refrigerated thin pizza crust dough

½   lb. sliced smoked chorizo sausage

½   cup thinly sliced sweet onion

2   tsp. olive oil

4   oz. cream cheese, softened

1   cup (4 oz.) shredded Monterey Jack cheese

¼   cup chopped fresh cilantro

½   tsp. lime zest

1   Tbsp. lime juice

1½ cups fresh or frozen (thawed) corn kernels

Fresh cilantro leaves

1. Preheat oven to 450°. Unroll dough; pat to an even thickness on a lightly greased baking sheet. Bake for 10 to 12 minutes or until lightly browned.

2. Sauté sausage and onion in hot olive oil until onion is tender; drain. Combine cream cheese and next 4 ingredients; spread over crust. Top with sausage mixture and corn kernels.

3. Bake at 450° for 8 to 10 minutes. Sprinkle with fresh cilantro leaves.

COMFORT FOOD WITH A KICK!

CHIPOTLE MAC AND CHEESE

makes: 12 servings   hands-on time: 20 min.   total time: 30 min.

1   (1-lb.) package elbow macaroni

¼   cup butter or margarine

¼   cup all-purpose flour

4   cups milk

4   cups (16 oz.) shredded sharp Cheddar cheese, divided

1   tsp. table salt

1   chipotle chile in adobo sauce, finely chopped (from 7-oz. can)

2   tsp. adobo sauce (from can of chipotle chiles)

⅓   cup chopped fresh cilantro

1½   cups fire-roasted chipotle tortilla chips, crushed (30 chips)

1. Preheat oven to 350°. Spray 13- x 9-inch glass baking dish with cooking spray. Prepare macaroni according to package directions, using minimum cook time.

2. Meanwhile, melt butter in a Dutch oven over low heat; stir in flour with whisk until blended. Cook and stir 1 minute. Gradually stir in milk with whisk; cook over medium heat 5 to 8 minutes, stirring constantly, until thickened. Remove from heat. Add 3 cups of cheese and salt; stir until smooth.

3. Stir cooked macaroni into cheese sauce. Stir in chipotle chile, adobo sauce, and cilantro. Spoon mixture into baking dish. Sprinkle with chips and remaining 1 cup cheese.

4. Bake, uncovered, at 350° for 5 to 10 minutes or until bubbly and cheese is melted.

The fire-roasted tortilla chip topping makes this mac 'n' cheese unique and gives it a flavorful crunch.

Taco Tip

LIME TORTILLA-CRUSTED CHICKEN TENDERS

makes: 6 servings hands-on time: 15 min. total time: 30 min.

2   large eggs

1   (2-lb.) package frozen chicken tenderloins, thawed

¾   tsp. table salt

¾   tsp. black pepper

¼   cup all-purpose flour

2¾   cups finely crushed lime-flavored tortilla chips

Garnishes: fresh cilantro sprigs, lime wedges

Serve these crunchy chicken fingers over white rice and with tomatillo salsa for dipping!

Taco Tip

1. Preheat oven to 425°. Whisk together eggs and 1 Tbsp. water until blended.

2. Sprinkle chicken with salt and pepper. Dredge chicken in flour; dip in egg mixture, and dredge in crushed tortilla chips. Place chicken on a lightly greased wire rack on an aluminum foil–lined baking sheet.

3. Bake at 425° for 15 to 20 minutes or until done.

Note: We tested with Tostitos® Hint of Lime Tortilla Chips.

A LITTLE MÁS

Make it a meal
by serving up some festive sides
and, of course, desserts!

TOMATO AND WATERMELON SALAD

makes: 4 to 6 servings hands-on time: 20 min. total time: 2 hours, 35 min.

Combine sweet, juicy watermelon chunks with fresh tomato, onion, and a red wine vinaigrette for a salad that's the essence of summer.

5   cups (¾-inch) seeded watermelon cubes

1½ lb. ripe tomatoes, cut into ¾-inch cubes

3   tsp. sugar

½   tsp. table salt

1   small red onion, quartered and thinly sliced

½   cup red wine vinegar

¼   cup extra virgin olive oil

Romaine lettuce leaves (optional)

Cracked black pepper

Garnish: basil leaves

1. Combine watermelon and tomatoes in a large bowl; sprinkle with sugar and salt, tossing to coat. Let stand 15 minutes.

2. Stir in onion, vinegar, and oil. Cover and chill 2 hours. Serve chilled with lettuce leaves, if desired. Sprinkle with cracked black pepper to taste.

GARDEN FRESH!

AVOCADO FRUIT SALAD

makes: 6 cups   hands-on time: 15 min.   total time: 1 hour, 15 min.

1   (24-oz.) jar refrigerated orange and grapefruit sections, drained, rinsed, and patted dry

1   (24-oz.) jar refrigerated tropical mixed fruit in light syrup, drained, rinsed, and patted dry

2   cups cubed fresh cantaloupe

1   medium-size ripe avocado, halved and cut into chunks

¼   cup chopped fresh mint

2   Tbsp. lime juice

1. Toss together all ingredients in a large bowl. Cover and chill 1 hour.

Note: We tested with Del Monte® SunFresh Citrus Salad and Del Monte® SunFresh Tropical Mixed Fruit in Light Syrup with Passion Fruit Juice.

You can prepare this salad a day ahead, but don't cut up the avocado until just before you serve it.

TACO TIP

HEARTS OF PALM AND JICAMA SALAD

makes: 6 to 8 servings hands-on time: 20 min. total time: 1 hour, 20 min.

1   (14.4-oz.) can hearts of palm, drained and rinsed

¼   red onion, thinly sliced

1   yellow bell pepper, diced

1   jicama, peeled and cut into ⅛-inch strips

1   jalapeño pepper, seeded and finely chopped

¼   cup chopped fresh cilantro

¼   cup fresh lime juice

¼   cup fresh orange juice

2   Tbsp. olive oil

1   tsp. table salt

½   tsp. ground cumin

1 avocado, diced

1. Cut hearts of palm crosswise into ½-inch slices. Stir together hearts of palm and next 10 ingredients in a large bowl. Cover and chill 1 to 8 hours. Stir in avocado just before serving.

Pick a jicama that's about the size of a large grapefruit, and use a vegetable peeler to remove the skin.

Taco Tip

MANGO TANGO

makes: 6 to 8 servings hands-on time: 20 min. total time: 2 hours, 20 min.

Mango Tango gets an added kick from minced jalapeño pepper that's added to this fruity side dish.

¼ **cup fresh lime juice**

3 **Tbsp. sugar**

1 **Tbsp. seeded and finely chopped jalapeño pepper**

2 **mangoes, peeled and sliced**

3 **large peaches, peeled and sliced**

3 **cups sliced assorted plums**

1 **Tbsp. chopped fresh mint**

1 **Tbsp. chopped fresh cilantro**

1. Stir together first 3 ingredients in a large bowl until sugar dissolves. Add mangoes and remaining ingredients, tossing to coat. Cover and chill 2 to 6 hours.

Taco Tip

Even though you could serve this right away, chilling this salad for a couple hours allows the lime, mint, and jalapeño flavors to permeate the fruit.

GRILLED SWEET POTATO SALAD

makes: 6 to 8 servings hands-on time: 20 min. total time: 40 min.

Vegetable cooking spray

2½ pounds small sweet potatoes

1 poblano pepper, seeded and diced

Cilantro Vinaigrette

1 (5-oz.) package fresh mâche

1 cup (4 oz.) crumbled queso fresco (fresh Mexican cheese)

½ cup sweetened dried cranberries

½ cup roasted and shelled pepitas (pumpkin seeds)

1. Coat cold cooking grate of grill with cooking spray, and place on grill. Preheat grill to 350° to 400° (medium-high) heat.

2. Peel sweet potatoes, and cut into ½-inch-thick rounds. Bring potatoes and water to cover to a boil in a large Dutch oven over medium-high heat; cook 5 to 6 minutes or until crisp-tender. Drain. Coat potatoes with cooking spray.

3. Grill potatoes, covered with grill lid, 8 to 10 minutes or until tender, turning occasionally. Gently toss warm potatoes with poblano and Cilantro Vinaigrette. Arrange mâche on a serving platter, and sprinkle with queso fresco and cranberries. Top with sweet potato mixture, and sprinkle with pumpkin seeds.

CILANTRO VINAIGRETTE

makes: 1 cup
hands-on time: 10 min.
total time: 10 min.

¼ cup red wine vinegar

2 Tbsp. chopped fresh cilantro

2 Tbsp. minced sweet onion

1 Tbsp. grated fresh ginger

2 Tbsp. honey

2 tsp. orange zest

2 tsp. Dijon mustard

½ tsp. table salt

½ cup canola oil

1. Whisk together all ingredients except for oil; add oil in a slow, steady stream, whisking constantly until smooth.

GRILLED JALAPEÑO LIME CORN ON THE COB

makes: 8 servings   hands-on time: 30 min.   total time: 30 min.

Add south-of-the-border flavor to buttery grilled corn with jalapeño peppers, cilantro, and lime juice.

8   ears fresh corn, husks removed

Vegetable cooking spray

½   cup butter, softened

1   jalapeño pepper, seeded and finely chopped

1   small garlic clove, pressed

1   Tbsp. lime zest

1   Tbsp. fresh lime juice

2   tsp. chopped fresh cilantro

Garnish: lime zest

1. Preheat grill to 350° to 400° (medium-high) heat. Coat corn lightly with cooking spray. Sprinkle with desired amount of salt and pepper. Grill corn, covered with grill lid, 15 minutes or until golden brown, turning occasionally.

2. Meanwhile, stir together butter and next 5 ingredients. Remove corn from grill, and cut into thirds. Serve corn with butter mixture.

Look for fresh corn with the husks already removed in the produce section to save you a few minutes of prep.

SPEED IT UP!

SPEEDY BLACK BEANS AND MEXICAN RICE

makes: 2 servings   hands-on time: 10 min.   total time: 10 min.

This hearty rice and bean dish is also perfect as a meatless main-dish choice, and it doubles perfectly.

1   (8.8-oz.) pouch ready-to-serve Mexican rice

1   (15-oz.) can black beans, drained and rinsed

1   (4.5-oz.) can chopped green chiles

2   Tbsp. chopped fresh cilantro

Toppings: sour cream, salsa, diced tomatoes, shredded Cheddar cheese

1. Cook rice according to package directions.

2. Combine black beans and green chiles in a microwave-safe bowl. Microwave at HIGH 90 seconds. Stir in rice and cilantro. Serve immediately with desired toppings.

Note: We tested with Rice-A-Roni Express Heat & Serve Mexican Rice.

Mexican Beef 'n' Rice: Substitute 1 lb. cooked lean ground beef for black beans. Substitute 1 cup salsa for green chiles. Prepare recipe as directed, omitting toppings. Serve with corn chips or in lettuce leaves, if desired. Makes 4 servings.

READY IN 10 MINUTES!

JALAPEÑO CORN SAUTE

makes: 6 servings hands-on time: 15 min. total time: 15 min.

¼ **cup butter or margarine**

4 **cups fresh whole kernel corn**

2 **jalapeño peppers, seeded and very finely chopped**

4 **garlic cloves, finely chopped**

½ **tsp. table salt**

1. Heat butter in a large skillet over medium-high heat until sizzling. Add remaining ingredients; cook 8 minutes, stirring occasionally, until corn is tender. Serve warm.

When seeding and chopping jalapeño peppers and other hot chile peppers, it's a good idea to wear rubber or plastic gloves. The capsaicin in the peppers can irritate skin and eyes.

Taco Tip

REFRIED BLACK BEANS

makes: 6 servings hands-on time: 13 min. total time: 27 min.

Bacon adds a wonderful smokiness to the beans, but you can make this a vegetarian dish by omitting the bacon and substituting 2 Tbsp. oil for the drippings.

4   bacon slices
1   large onion, chopped
2   garlic cloves, minced
1   tsp. ground cumin
½   tsp. ground chipotle chili pepper
¼   tsp. table salt
2   (15-oz.) cans black beans, drained

6   Tbsp. fresh jalapeño pepper slices
¼   cup loosely packed fresh cilantro leaves
6   Tbsp. crumbled queso fresco (fresh Mexican cheese)
6   lime wedges

1. Cook bacon in a large nonstick skillet over medium-high heat 4 to 5 minutes or until crisp; remove bacon, and drain on paper towels, reserving 2 Tbsp. drippings in skillet. Crumble bacon.

2. Sauté onion and next 4 ingredients in hot drippings over medium heat 5 minutes or until tender.

3. Add beans to skillet. Mash beans over medium heat, and cook 5 to 10 minutes or to desired consistency, adding ¼ cup water, if necessary. Remove from heat; sprinkle with bacon, jalapeño pepper slices, cilantro, and cheese. Serve with lime wedges.

PRONTO REFRIED BEANS

makes: 6 servings   hands-on time: 10 min.   total time: 40 min.

A sprinkle of queso fresco, a fresh white Mexican cheese, adds traditional flavor to this quick side dish. You can buy it at your local supercenter or Hispanic market.

1   (14½-oz.) can stewed Mexican-style tomatoes, undrained

1   (31-oz.) can refried beans

1   tsp. chili powder

½   tsp. cumin

1   cup (4 oz.) crumbled queso fresco (fresh Mexican cheese)

Garnish: cilantro sprigs

1. Preheat oven to 350°. Stir together first 4 ingredients. Place bean mixture into a lightly greased 2-qt. baking dish. Sprinkle evenly with queso fresco.

2. Bake at 350° for 25 minutes or until thoroughly heated. Let stand 5 minutes before serving.

Taco Tip

Make these extra special by preparing in individual oven-proof ramekins. Bake about 20 minutes or until thoroughly heated.

MELTY & CHEESY!

TEX-MEX MASHED POTATO BAKE

makes: 6 to 8 servings hands-on time: 25 min. total time: 1 hour

These potatoes get a spicy kick with the addition of chorizo sausage, green chiles, and pepper Jack cheese. Mashed potatoes will never be boring again!

4   lb. baking potatoes

3   tsp. table salt, divided

1¼   cups warm buttermilk

½   cup warm milk

¼   cup melted butter

½   tsp. black pepper

1   (4.5-oz.) can chopped green chiles

1¼   cups (5 oz.) shredded pepper Jack cheese

½   cup finely chopped cooked chorizo sausage

1. Preheat oven to 350°. Peel potatoes; cut into 2-inch pieces. Bring potatoes, 2 tsp. salt, and water to cover to a boil in a large Dutch oven over medium-high heat; boil 20 minutes or until tender. Drain. Return potatoes to Dutch oven, reduce heat to low, and cook, stirring occasionally, 3 to 5 minutes or until potatoes are dry.

2. Mash potatoes with a potato masher to desired consistency. Stir in buttermilk, milk, butter, pepper, and remaining 1 tsp. salt, stirring just until blended.

3. Stir in green chiles, pepper Jack cheese, and chorizo sausage, and spoon the mixture into a lightly greased 2½-qt. baking dish or 8 (10-oz.) ramekins. Bake at 350° for 35 minutes.

PUMPKIN SEED SHORTBREAD

makes: 4 dozen cookies hands-on time: 25 min. total time: 2 hours, 40 min.

1½ **cups butter, softened**

1   **cup sugar**

½   **tsp. vanilla extract**

3½ **cups all-purpose flour**

¼   **tsp. table salt**

¾   **cup roasted, salted, and shelled pepitas (pumpkin seeds), toasted, divided**

Vegetable cooking spray

Use metal cookie cutters to cut through pumpkin seeds easily in this dough.

Taco Tip

1. Beat butter, sugar, and vanilla at medium speed with an electric mixer for 1 minute, or mix with spoon, until well blended. Stir in flour, salt, and ½ cup of the pumpkin seeds. Shape dough into a ball; flatten to 1-inch thickness. Cover; refrigerate about 2 hours.

2. Preheat oven to 350°. Spray baking sheets with cooking spray. Roll dough to ¼-inch thickness on a lightly floured surface. Cut into desired shapes with 2-inch cookie cutters. Place cutouts on baking sheets about 1 inch apart. Sprinkle with remaining ¼ cup pumpkin seeds, pressing gently into cutouts.

3. Bake at 350° for 10 to 12 minutes or until set. Immediately remove from baking sheets to cooling racks.

CARAMEL APPLE WEDGES

makes: 16 servings   hands-on time: 25 min.   total time: 55 min.

Parchment paper

2   Granny Smith apples, peeled, each cut into 8 wedges

1   Tbsp. lemon juice

¼   cup sugar

½   tsp. apple pie spice

3   refrigerated piecrusts, softened as directed on box

1   egg, slightly beaten

1   Tbsp. sugar

¾   cup caramel bits

1   Tbsp. milk

1. Preheat oven to 425°. Line 2 baking sheets with parchment paper. Toss apples with lemon juice in a medium bowl. Mix ¼ cup sugar and apple pie spice in a small bowl; sprinkle over apples, tossing to coat.

2. Unroll piecrusts on a lightly floured surface. Roll each crust into a 10-inch round. Using 4-inch round cutter, cut out 16 rounds. Place 8 rounds on each cookie sheet. Place 1 apple wedge off-center on each round. Brush edges of rounds with egg. Wrap and press edges together; seal with a fork. Brush tops with remaining egg; sprinkle with 1 Tbsp. sugar.

3. Bake at 425° for 14 to 16 minutes or until crust is golden brown. Remove from baking sheets to cooling rack; cool at least 10 minutes.

4. Microwave caramels and milk in a small microwave-safe bowl, uncovered, at HIGH 1 minute; stir. Continue to microwave at 30-second intervals, stirring until caramels melt and mixture is smooth. Drizzle caramel over wedges.

Taco Tip

For extra decadence, sprinkle wedges with chopped pecans after drizzling with caramel.

DESSERT
EMPANADAS!

CARAMEL PEANUT POPCORN SQUARES

makes: 24 servings   hands-on time: 20 min.   total time: 2 hours, 10 min.

Popcorn and peanuts are the star ingredients in these bars. A gooey marshmallow layer holds it all together.

1   (18-oz.) package refrigerated peanut butter cookie dough

3½ cups miniature marshmallows

1   (3-oz.) bag butter-flavored microwave popcorn, popped (8 cups)

1   cup lightly salted dry-roasted peanuts

1   (10-oz.) bag peanut butter chips (1⅔ cups)

⅔   cup light corn syrup

¼   cup butter or margarine

1   cup semisweet chocolate chips (6 oz.)

1. Preheat oven to 350°. Lightly grease a 13- x 9-inch pan. Press dough evenly in bottom of pan with floured fingers to form crust.

2. Bake at 350° for 14 to 16 minutes or until light golden brown. Sprinkle marshmallows over crust. Bake 3 more minutes or until marshmallows are puffed but not browned.

3. Meanwhile, mix popcorn and peanuts in a large bowl; set aside. Microwave peanut butter chips, corn syrup, and butter in a microwave-safe bowl, uncovered, at HIGH 1 to 2 minutes, stirring every 30 seconds, until peanut butter chips melt and mixture is smooth. Pour over popcorn mixture; stir to coat completely. Immediately press mixture over marshmallows in an even layer, using the back of a spoon.

4. Microwave chocolate chips in a microwave-safe bowl, uncovered, at HIGH 1 minute. Continue to microwave at 30-second intervals, stirring until chocolate melts and mixture is smooth. Drizzle melted chocolate over bars. Cool on cooling rack 1 hour. Refrigerate 30 minutes or until set. Cut into squares.

OVEN-BAKED CHURROS

makes: 3 dozen hands-on time: 15 min. total time: 30 min.

1   (17.3-oz.) package frozen puff pastry sheets, thawed

Parchment paper

¼   cup sugar

1   tsp. ground cinnamon

¼   cup melted butter

1. Preheat oven to 450°. Unfold and cut puff pastry sheets in half lengthwise, and cut each half crosswise into 1-inch-wide strips. Place strips on a lightly greased parchment paper–lined baking sheet. Bake 10 minutes or until golden brown.

2. Meanwhile, combine sugar and cinnamon. Remove pastry strips from oven, and dip in butter; roll in cinnamon-sugar mixture. Let stand on a wire rack 5 minutes or until dry.

ICED MEXICAN CHOCOLATE SIPPER

makes: about 7 cups hands-on time: 10 min. total time: 10 min.

2   (14-oz.) containers premium chocolate ice cream

2   cups milk

¾   to 1 tsp. ground cinnamon

½   tsp. orange zest

1   cup bourbon

Garnishes: orange zest curls, sweetened whipped cream, ground cinnamon

1. Pulse first 4 ingredients in a blender until smooth. Stir in bourbon. Serve immediately over ice.

DESSERT DUO!

CARAMEL CREAM CHEESE FLAN

makes: 8 servings hands-on time: 25 min. total time: 7 hours, 15 min.

1½ **cups sugar, divided**

7 **egg yolks**

1 **(14-oz.) can sweetened condensed milk**

1 **(12-oz.) can evaporated milk**

¾ **cup milk**

1½ **tsp. vanilla extract**

⅛ **tsp. table salt**

4 **egg whites**

1 **(8-oz.) package cream cheese, softened**

1. Preheat oven to 350°. Cook 1 cup sugar in a 9-inch round cake pan over medium heat, stirring occasionally, 5 minutes or until sugar melts and turns golden brown. Remove pan from heat, and let stand 5 minutes. (Sugar will harden.)

2. Meanwhile, whisk together egg yolks and next 5 ingredients in a large bowl.

3. Process egg whites, cream cheese, and remaining ½ cup sugar in a blender until smooth. Add 2 cups egg yolk mixture, and process until smooth. Stir egg white mixture into remaining egg yolk mixture until blended. Pour custard over caramelized sugar in pan.

4. Place cake pan in a large shallow pan. Add hot water to large pan to depth of one-third up sides of cake pan.

5. Bake at 350° for 50 to 60 minutes or until a knife inserted into center of flan comes out clean. Remove pan from water; cool completely on a wire rack (about 2 hours). Cover and chill 4 hours to 2 days.

6. Run a knife around edge of flan to loosen; invert onto a serving plate. (Once inverted, the flan will take about 30 seconds to slip from the pan. Be sure to use a serving plate with a lip to catch the extra caramel sauce.)

MEXICAN CHOCOLATE SHEET CAKE

makes: 12 servings hands-on time: 20 min. total time: 2 hours, 35 min.

This moist, tender cake is a spin on the traditional chocolate sheet cake, with hints of cinnamon and coffee in both the cake and frosting.

- 2 **cups all-purpose flour**
- 2 **cups sugar**
- ¼ **cup unsweetened cocoa**
- 1¼ **tsp. ground cinnamon, divided**
- 1 **tsp. baking soda**
- ¼ **tsp. table salt**
- 1 **cup butter or margarine, melted**
- 1 **cup strong brewed coffee (room temperature)**
- ½ **cup buttermilk**
- 1 **tsp. vanilla extract**
- 2 **large eggs, beaten**
- 2 **tsp. instant coffee granules**
- 2 **tsp. warm water**
- 1 **(1-lb.) container milk chocolate frosting**

Frozen whipped topping, thawed

Additional ground cinnamon, if desired

1. Preheat oven to 350°. Grease 13- x 9-inch pan with shortening; lightly flour. Mix flour, sugar, cocoa, 1 tsp. cinnamon, baking soda, and salt. Add butter, brewed coffee, buttermilk, vanilla, and eggs; mix with wire whisk until well blended. Pour batter into pan.

2. Bake at 350° for 40 to 44 minutes or until toothpick inserted in center comes out clean. Cool on cooling rack 30 minutes.

3. Mix coffee granules and warm water in a small bowl. Mix frosting, remaining ¼ tsp. cinnamon, and coffee mixture in a medium bowl until smooth. Spread frosting over warm cake. Cool 1 hour or until cake is completely cooled. Serve with a dollop of whipped topping, and sprinkle with additional cinnamon.

TRES LECHES CAKE

makes: 16 servings hands-on time: 25 min. total time: 3 hours, including frosting

This exceptional dessert takes a little extra effort, but it's worth it. The combination of textures—tender cake, fluffy frosting, and a pool of creamy sauce—will delight your family and friends.

7   large eggs, separated
½   cup butter, softened
1   cup sugar
2½   cups all-purpose flour
1   tsp. baking powder
½   tsp. table salt
1   cup milk
1   tsp. vanilla extract

1   (14-oz.) can sweetened condensed milk
1   (12-oz.) can evaporated milk
¾   cup whipping cream
Fluffy Frosting
Garnish: lemon zest

1. Preheat oven to 350°. Beat egg yolks, butter, and sugar at medium speed with an electric mixer 2 minutes or until mixture is creamy.

2. Combine flour, baking powder, and salt. Add to egg yolk mixture alternately with milk, beginning and ending with flour mixture. Beat at low speed just until blended after each addition. Stir in vanilla. Beat egg whites until stiff; fold gently into batter. Pour batter into a greased and floured 13- x 9-inch pan. Bake at 350° for 25 minutes or until a wooden pick inserted in center comes out clean. Let stand 10 minutes.

3. Pierce top of cake several times with a small wooden skewer. Stir together condensed milk, evaporated milk, and cream; gradually pour and spread over warm cake. Let stand 2 hours; cover and chill overnight, if desired. Spread top of cake with Fluffy Frosting before serving.

FLUFFY FROSTING

makes enough for 1 cake
hands-on time: 15 min.
total time: 15 min.

6   egg whites
1   cup sugar
1   cup light corn syrup
1   Tbsp. fresh lemon juice

1. Pour water to a depth of 1½ inches into bottom of double boiler over medium-high heat; bring to a boil. Reduce heat to a gentle boil. Place egg whites and sugar in top of double boiler. Beat at high speed with an electric mixer 5 to 7 minutes or until stiff peaks form. Gradually pour in corn syrup and lemon juice, beating 7 minutes or until spreading consistency.

MEXICAN CHOCOLATE POUND CAKE

makes: 16 servings   hands-on time: 25 min.   total time: 3 hours, 15 min., including chocolate sauce

1   (8-oz.) package semi-sweet chocolate baking squares, chopped

1   cup butter, softened

1½   cups granulated sugar

4   large eggs

½   cup chocolate syrup

2   tsp. vanilla extract

2½   cups all-purpose flour

1   tsp. ground cinnamon

¼   tsp. baking soda

⅛   tsp. table salt

1   cup buttermilk

Powdered sugar (optional)

Garnishes: Mexican Chocolate Sauce, toasted sliced almonds

1. Preheat oven to 325°. Microwave chocolate baking squares in a microwave-safe bowl at HIGH 1 minute and 15 seconds or until melted and smooth, stirring at 15-second intervals. Beat butter at medium speed with a heavy-duty electric stand mixer 2 minutes or until creamy. Gradually add granulated sugar, beating 5 to 7 minutes or until light and fluffy. Add eggs, 1 at a time, beating just until yellow disappears after each addition. Stir in melted chocolate, chocolate syrup, and vanilla until smooth.

2. Combine flour and next 3 ingredients; add to butter mixture alternately with buttermilk, beginning and ending with flour mixture. Beat at low speed just until blended after each addition. Pour batter into a greased and floured 10-inch (14-cup) tube pan.

3. Bake at 325° for 1 hour and 10 minutes or until a long wooden pick inserted in center of cake comes out clean. Cool in pan on a wire rack 10 to 15 minutes; remove from pan to wire rack, and let cool completely (about 1 hour and 30 minutes). Sprinkle with powdered sugar, if desired. Serve with Mexican Chocolate Sauce.

MEXICAN CHOCOLATE SAUCE

makes: 1½ cups
hands-on time: 10 min.
total time: 10 min.

1   (8-oz.) package semisweet chocolate baking squares, chopped

¾   cup whipping cream

2   tsp. light brown sugar

¼   tsp. ground cinnamon

¼   tsp. almond extract

Pinch of table salt

1   Tbsp. butter

1. Cook all ingredients, except for butter, in a small saucepan over low heat, whisking occasionally, 3 to 4 minutes or until mixture is smooth and chocolate is melted. Remove from heat. Whisk in butter until melted. Serve immediately.

KEY LIME ICEBOX CAKE

makes: 8 to 10 servings hands-on time: 25 min. total time: 9 hours, 25 min.

¾ **cup granulated sugar**

¼ **cup cornstarch**

⅛ **tsp. kosher salt**

4 **large egg yolks**

2 **cups half-and-half**

3 **Tbsp. butter**

2 **Tbsp. Key lime zest***

½ **cup fresh Key lime juice***

45 **graham cracker squares**

1 **cup whipping cream**

¼ **cup powdered sugar**

1. Whisk together first 3 ingredients in a heavy saucepan. Whisk together egg yolks and half-and-half in a bowl. Gradually whisk egg mixture into sugar mixture; bring to a boil over medium heat, whisking constantly. Boil, whisking constantly, 1 minute; remove from heat. Whisk in butter and zest until butter melts. Gradually whisk in juice just until blended. Pour into a metal bowl, and place bowl on ice. Let stand, stirring occasionally, 8 to 10 minutes or until custard is cold and slightly thickened.

2. Meanwhile, line bottom and sides of an 8-inch square pan with plastic wrap, allowing 4 inches to extend over sides. Place 9 graham crackers, with sides touching, in a single layer in bottom of pan to form a large square. (Crackers will not completely cover bottom.)

3. Spoon about ¾ cup cold custard over crackers; spread to edge of crackers. Repeat layers 3 times with crackers and remaining custard, ending with custard; top with remaining 9 crackers. Pull sides of plastic wrap tightly over cake; freeze in pan 8 hours.

4. Lift cake from pan, and place on a platter; discard plastic wrap. Cover loosely; let stand 1 hour.

5. Beat whipping cream at high speed with an electric mixer until foamy; gradually add powdered sugar, beating until soft peaks form. Spread on top of cake.

* Regular (Persian) lime zest and juice may be substituted.

Add the lime juice after you've fully cooked the custard to let the cornstarch thicken the mixture properly.

Taco Tip

MEXICAN CHOCOLATE ICE-CREAM PIE

makes: 8 servings   hands-on time: 30 min.   total time: 10 hours, 50 min.

A crisp, over-the-rim graham cracker crust spiked with ground cinnamon and red pepper adds a spicy cowboy kick to this show-stopping Mexican Chocolate Ice-cream Pie.

- **3** cups cinnamon graham cracker crumbs (about 22 whole crackers), divided
- **½** cup butter, melted
- **¼** tsp. ground red pepper
- **1** (4-oz.) semisweet chocolate baking bar, finely chopped
- **1** (3.5-oz.) package roasted glazed pecan pieces
- **1** pt. chocolate ice cream, softened
- **1** pt. coffee ice cream, softened
- **1** cup whipping cream
- **¼** cup coffee liqueur

1. Preheat oven to 350°. Stir together 2½ cups cinnamon graham cracker crumbs and next 2 ingredients; firmly press mixture on bottom and up sides of a lightly greased 9-inch pie plate. Bake 10 to 12 minutes or until lightly browned. Cool completely on a wire rack (about 30 minutes).

2. Stir together semisweet chocolate, pecan pieces, and remaining ½ cup cinnamon graham cracker crumbs. Reserve ½ cup chocolate-pecan mixture to top pie.

3. Spread chocolate ice cream in bottom of prepared crust; top with remaining chocolate-pecan mixture. Freeze 30 minutes. Spread coffee ice cream over chocolate mixture. Cover and freeze 8 hours.

4. Beat whipping cream and coffee liqueur at medium speed with an electric mixer until stiff peaks form. Spread whipped cream mixture over pie; sprinkle with reserved ½ cup chocolate-pecan mixture. Cover and freeze 1 hour or until whipped cream is firm. Let stand 10 to 15 minutes before serving.

TACO TALK

ADOBO SAUCE
A Mexican seasoning paste or sauce made from ground sesame seeds, chiles, herbs, and vinegar. Find it in the Mexican foods section of your grocery.

AGUA FRESCAS
Means fresh water in Spanish. Agua frescas is a water-based non-alcoholic drink flavored with a combination of fruit, flowers, or seeds that have been blended with sugar for sweetness.

ANCHO CHILE PEPPER
A dried, deep reddish-brown poblano chile pepper that's broad at the stem end and tapers to a rounded tip. Its flavor ranges from mild to pungent.

AVOCADO
A tropical fruit grown mostly in Florida and California that's round or pear-shaped, has green to dark purplish skin, buttery-smooth yellow to green meat, and a large pit. This fruit is known for its lush, buttery texture and mild, nutlike flavor. It's served peeled, sliced, or pureed in salads and dips and is the primary ingredient in guacamole. Some avocados are rock hard when purchased. Place these in a paper bag and leave at room temperature; they'll soften in 2 to 5 days. Refrigerate ripe avocadoes and use within a few days. Avocados don't freeze well. The easiest way to "pit" an avocado is to slice all the way around the pit and through both ends of the fruit with a chef's knife. Then twist the halves in opposite directions, and pull them apart. Tap the pit sharply with the knife, and twist the blade to lift the pit.

BURRITO
A Mexican or Tex-Mex specialty consisting of a flour tortilla folded and rolled around savory fillings such as shredded meat, refried beans, shredded cheese, lettuce, tomatoes, and sour cream.

CARNE ASADA
Grilled meat, usually sliced thin and served on tortillas.

CARNITA
A dish made of pork that's been braised or roasted until tender. The meat can be a dish by itself, or it can be used in tacos, burritos, and other dishes. We've simmered ours in a slow cooker and dressed it up as an appetizer in Pork Carnita Nachos (page 38), topping it off with peppers, cheese, and salsa.

CHILI POWDER
A powdered seasoning mixture of dried chiles, garlic, oregano, cumin, coriander, and cloves. It's used most often in Southwestern and Mexican dishes.

CHILI RELLENOS
A Mexican dish of mild roasted chiles stuffed with cheese, then dipped in an egg batter and fried.

CHIMICHANGA
A Mexican deep-fried burrito filled with chicken, beef, or pork, refried beans, and cheese, and topped with sour cream, salsa, pico de gallo, guacamole, and shredded cheese.

CHIPOTLE CHILE PEPPER

A smoked jalapeño pepper available dried, canned, and pickled. If dried, it has a dark red color with a wrinkled skin and a smoky, slightly sweet, hot flavor. They're typically canned in adobo sauce, which is used as a seasoning along with chipotles. Chipotles are added to stews and sauces; the picked variety often is eaten as appetizers.

CHORIZO

A ground pork sausage flavored with garlic, chili powder, and other spices, often used in Mexican and Spanish dishes. Mexican chorizo is made with fresh pork, and the casing is usually removed before the sausage is cooked.

CILANTRO

The fresh, bright green, lacy leaves from the coriander plant have pungent fragrance and taste. Many describe the flavor as (pleasantly) soapy tasting. Cilantro is definitely an acquired taste, and strong opinions prevail; people either love it or loathe it. Find it year-round in most supermarkets, and store it in the refrigerator for up to 1 week in a plastic bag.

EMPANADAS

Mexican and Spanish deep-fried turnovers with pastry crusts and fillings of meat, vegetables, or fruit.

ENCHILADAS

A Mexican dish consisting of a soft corn tortilla wrapped around a meat or cheese filling. Enchiladas are typically served hot and topped with red sauce, cheese, guacamole, or sour cream.

FAJITAS

A Mexican-American dish traditionally made from skirt or flank steak that has been marinated in a mixture of oil, lime juice, pepper, and garlic before being grilled. The grilled meat is cut into thin strips, wrapped in a flour tortilla, and accompanied with a variety of toppings, including grilled onions and bell peppers, guacamole, salsa, refried beans, and sour cream.

GUACAMOLE

An avocado dish that's a popular Mexican dip, sauce, side dish, or salad. Guacamole is made from mashed avocado mixed with lemon or lime juice, and variations often include chopped tomato, green onions, chile peppers, and cilantro. Guacamole turns brown when exposed to air for very long, so it's best served within an hour of making. Store guacamole in the refrigerator with plastic wrap pressed directly on the surface to help prevent browning. If, despite your efforts, browning does occur, don't panic; just scrape off the browned part before serving.

HABANERO CHILE PEPPER

This small, squatty, very hot chili pepper has green to bright orange skin and is used for making spicy sauces. It is one of the hottest peppers on the Scoville scale, the scale that measures the pungency of peppers. We recommend that you wear gloves when handling habaneros.

JALAPEÑO PEPPER

A smooth-skinned chile pepper with a hot to very hot, green vegetable flavor and dark green color. This short, tapering chile is usually about 2 inches long and ¾ to 1 inch in diameter. When seeding a jalapeño, it's best to wear rubber gloves because the seeds and veins are also hot and can burn your hands. Jalapeños can be purchased fresh or canned.

JICAMA

A round, tropical root vegetable, also known as the Mexican potato. Jicama has a thin, sandy brown skin that should be peeled before it's used; the white, crisp flesh has a sweet, nutty flavor. It's most often eaten raw with dips or in salad. Fresh jicamas can be stored, unwrapped, in the vegetable bin of your refrigerator for up to 3 weeks.

LECHE

A Spanish term for milk.

MARGARITA

A cocktail made of tequila, lime juice, and an orange-flavored liqueur such as Triple Sec or Cointreau. Margaritas are typically served in a stemmed glass with a large bowl, and the rim might be dipped in lime juice and coated with salt. To make slushy, frozen margaritas, blend the cocktail mixture with crushed ice.

NACHOS

A crisp tortilla or tortilla chips topped with melted cheese and chile peppers. Nachos might also be topped with salsa, sour cream, or refried beans. They're usually served as an appetizer.

PICADILLO

A Spanish hash made from ground pork and beef or veal, and tomatoes, garlic, and onions. In Mexico, picadillo is used as a stuffing. We've used it as a stuffing in Taquitos with Pork Picadillo (page 153).

PICO DE GALLO

A zesty relish made of chopped tomatoes, onions, bell pepper, jalapeño, and cucumbers. Jicama and oranges may also be added. It's popular throughout Mexico and South America.

POBLANO CHILE

A large, dark green fresh chile pepper with a rich, mild-to-hot flavor. Poblanos are often stuffed with cheese for chiles rellenos. They're available fresh, canned, or dried; when dried, poblanos are called ancho chile peppers.

POZOLE

A soup or stew with pork, hominy, chile, and vegetables.

QUESADILLA

A flour tortilla folded in half over some combination of cheese, meat, chicken, or refried beans. The filled and folded quesadilla is toasted, grilled, or fried, and served with salsa or sour cream.

QUESO

A Spanish term for cheese.

QUESO FRESCO

A soft, mild unaged Mexican cheese.

QUESO FUNDIDO

Melted cheese. Think of it as a Mexican cheese fondue.

REFRIED BEANS

A popular Mexican side dish or filling of mashed and fried red beans, black beans, or pinto beans. The beans can be eaten plain or spread on tortillas. They're sold canned in most supermarkets.

SALSA

This term usually refers to a Mexican sauce made from tomatoes flavored with cilantro, chiles, and onions. Salsa is commonly served with meat, poultry, or fish to pump up the flavor.

SERRANO CHILE

A short, tapered chile with a green or orange-yellow color, thick flesh, and very hot flavor. It's found fresh in Mexican markets and some supermarkets; it's also available canned, pickled, or packed in oil. Serrano chiles are especially tasty in guacamole and salsa.

SOPAIPILLA

A crisp, deep-fried Mexican dessert pastry that's puffy with a hollow center. Sopaipillas are usually served with honey or a cinnamon-flavored syrup.

TACO

A type of Mexican "sandwich" made with small folded corn or flour tortillas that are crisp (deep-fried) or soft. The taco shells are filled with beef, pork, chicken, chorizo sausage, or refried beans, and topped with chopped tomatoes, shredded lettuce, shredded cheese, chopped onions, guacamole, sour cream, and salsa.

TAQUERIA

A Spanish word meaning taco shop or place that makes tacos.

TAQUITOS

A Mexican dish consisting of a small tortilla rolled around a filling of meat and cheese and deep-fried. Our taquitos are filled with pork and Monterey Jack cheese (page 153) .

TAMALE

A popular Mexican dish of chopped, chili-flavored meat that's coated with masa dough, wrapped in a softened corn husk, and steamed until the masa is cooked; to eat, just peel back the corn husk. Sometimes tamales are sweet; these usually have a fruit-filled center.

TOMATILLO

Resembling a small green tomato partially wrapped in a wrinkled parchment-like husk, tomatillos are an essential ingredient in Mexican and Tex-Mex foods, especially green salsa. They have a firm, crisp, pale yellow flesh and a tart, acidic, lemony, herbal flavor. Although tomatillos are not related to the tomato, they are sometimes called Mexican green tomatoes and are sold in Latin-Mexican markets and some supermarkets. Look for those with dry, tight-fitting husks for longest shelf life, and keep in a plastic bag in the refrigerator for up to 2 weeks.

TORTILLA

Flat, thin, round, unleavened Mexican bread made from either corn flour (masa) or wheat flour. Tortillas are patted out by hand or pressed in a tortilla press, and baked on a griddle or in a skillet. They are the basis of countless classic Mexican dishes such as tacos, enchiladas, and burritos. Both corn and flour tortillas are sold pre-packaged in either the refrigerated section or in the bread aisle of most supermarkets.

TOSTADA

A crisp-fried tortilla topped with refried beans, shredded chicken or beef, and topped with lettuce, cheese, tomatoes, sour cream, guacamole, and salsa.

TRES LECHES CAKE

Spanish meaning three milks cake. A tres leches cake is typically a sponge cake soaked in three kinds of milks. Our version (page 207) uses sweetened condensed milk, evaporated milk, and whipping cream, creating a creamy sauce when the cake is cut.

METRIC EQUIVALENTS

The information in the following charts is provided to help cooks outside the United States successfully use the recipes in this book. All equivalents are approximate.

Equivalents for Different Types of Ingredients

Standard Cup	Fine Powder (ex. flour)	Grain (ex. rice)	Granular (ex. sugar)	Liquid Solids (ex. butter)	Liquid (ex. milk)
1	140 g	150 g	190 g	200 g	240 ml
¾	105 g	113 g	143 g	150 g	180 ml
⅔	93 g	100 g	125 g	133 g	160 ml
½	70 g	75 g	95 g	100 g	120 ml
⅓	47 g	50 g	63 g	67 g	80 ml
¼	35 g	38 g	48 g	50 g	60 ml
⅛	18 g	19 g	24 g	25 g	30 ml

Liquid Ingredients by Volume

¼ tsp	=						1 ml
½ tsp	=						2 ml
1 tsp	=						5 ml
3 tsp	=	1 Tbsp	=	½ fl oz	=		15 ml
2 Tbsp	=	⅛ cup	=	1 fl oz	=		30 ml
4 Tbsp	=	¼ cup	=	2 fl oz	=		60 ml
5⅓ Tbsp	=	⅓ cup	=	3 fl oz	=		80 ml
8 Tbsp	=	½ cup	=	4 fl oz	=		120 ml
10⅔ Tbsp	=	⅔ cup	=	5 fl oz	=		160 ml
12 Tbsp	=	¾ cup	=	6 fl oz	=		180 ml
16 Tbsp	=	1 cup	=	8 fl oz	=		240 ml
1 pt	=	2 cups	=	16 fl oz	=		480 ml
1 qt	=	4 cups	=	32 fl oz	=		960 ml
				33 fl oz	=	1000 ml	= 1 l

Dry Ingredients by Weight
(To convert ounces to grams, multiply the number of ounces by 30.)

1 oz	=	¹⁄₁₆ lb	=	30 g
4 oz	=	¼ lb	=	120 g
8 oz	=	½ lb	=	240 g
12 oz	=	¾ lb	=	360 g
16 oz	=	1 lb	=	480 g

Length
(To convert inches to centimeters, multiply the number of inches by 2.5.)

1 in	=			2.5 cm
6 in	=	½ ft	=	15 cm
12 in	=	1 ft	=	30 cm
36 in	=	3 ft = 1 yd	=	90 cm
40 in	=			100 cm = 1 m

Cooking/Oven Temperatures

	Fahrenheit	Celsius	Gas Mark
Freeze Water	32° F	0° C	
Room Temp.	68° F	20° C	
Boil Water	212° F	100° C	
Bake	325° F	160° C	3
	350° F	180° C	4
	375° F	190° C	5
	400° F	200° C	6
	425° F	220° C	7
	450° F	230° C	8
Broil			Grill

INDEX

ISBN-13: 978-0-8487-4291-1
ISBN-10: 0-8487-4291-5
Library of Congress Control Number: 2013957604

Printed in the United States of America
First Printing 2014

Oxmoor House
Vice President, Brand Publishing: Laura Sappington
Editorial Director: Leah McLaughlin
Creative Director: Felicity Keane
Brand Manager: Katie McHugh
Senior Editor: Rebecca Brennan
Managing Editor: Elizabeth Tyler Austin
Assistant Managing Editor: Jeanne de Lathouder

Taco Night!
Editor: Allison E. Cox
Art Director: Christopher Rhoads
Project Editor: Emily Chappell Connolly
Assistant Designer: Allison Sperando Potter
Executive Food Director: Grace Parisi
Assistant Test Kitchen Manager:
    Alyson Moreland Haynes
Recipe Developers and Testers: Wendy Ball, R.D.;
    Tamara Goldis, R.D.; Stefanie Maloney; Callie Nash;
    Karen Rankin; Leah Van Deren
Food Stylists: Victoria E. Cox, Margaret Monroe Dickey,
    Catherine Crowell Steele
Photography Director: Jim Bathie
Senior Photographer: Hélène Dujardin
Senior Photo Stylist: Kay E. Clarke
Photo Stylist: Mindi Shapiro Levine
Assistant Photo Stylist: Mary Louise Menendez
Senior Production Manager: Susan Chodakiewicz
Assistant Production Manager: Diane Rose Keener

Contributors
Editor: Cathy Wesler
Copy Editors: Rhonda Lee Lother, *Marra*thon
    Production Services
Proofreader: Lucia Carruthers
Indexer: Nanette Cardon
Fellows: Ali Carruba, Elizabeth Laseter, Amy Pinney,
    Frances Higginbotham, Madison Taylor Pozzo,
    Deanna Sakal, April Smitherman, Megan Thompson,
    Tonya West
Food Stylist: Charlotte Autry
Photographer: Johnny Autry
Photo Stylist: Charlotte Autry

Time Home Entertainment Inc.
Publisher: Jim Childs
Vice President, Brand & Digital Strategy:
    Steven Sandonato
Vice President, Finance: Vandana Patel
Executive Director, Marketing Services: Carol Pittard
Executive Director, Retail & Special Sales: Tom Mifsud
Executive Publishing Director: Joy Butts
Publishing Director: Megan Pearlman
Director, Bookazine Development & Marketing:
    Laura Adam
Associate General Counsel: Helen Wan